ISRAEL

TITLES IN THE MODERN NATIONS OF THE WORLD SERIES INCLUDE:

Afghanistan

Australia

Austria

Brazil

Canada

China

Cuba

Czech Republic

England

Ethiopia

France

Germany

Greece

Haiti

Hungary

India

Iran

Ireland

Italy

Japan

Jordan

Kenya

Lebanon

Mexico

Nigeria

Norway

Pakistan

Peru

Poland

Russia

Saudi Arabia

Scotland

Somalia

South Africa

South Korea

Spain

Sweden

Switzerland

Taiwan

Thailand

United States

Vietnam

ISRAEL

BY LAUREL CORONA

LUCENT
BOOKS®

THOMSON
™
GALE

San Diego • Detroit • New York • San Francisco • Cleveland
New Haven, Conn. • Waterville, Maine • London • Munich

To Eden, Nadav, and Eli
and
Yarden, Amit, Gal, and Maya

With hope that they may grow up in an Israel at peace

LIBRARY OF CONGRESS CATALOGING-IN-PUBLICATION DATA

Corona, Laurel, 1949–
    Israel / by Laurel Corona.
        p. cm. — (Modern nations of the world)
Summary: Discusses the vision of a Jewish homeland, the founding of Israel, and the
struggles and dangers of daily life in Israel.
    ISBN 1-59018-115-8 (hardback : alk. paper)
    1. Israel—Description and travel—Juvenile literature. 2. Israel—History—20th cen-
tury—Juvenile literature. [1. Israel.] I. Title. II. Series.
    DS118 .C83 2003
    956.94—dc21

                                                 2002010428

Printed in the United States of America

CONTENTS

INTRODUCTION

A Nation United and Divided

Israel is a tiny country, a sliver along the eastern Mediterranean coast, but no country, even those many times its size, has generated more controversy. The controversy swirls at many levels; in fact, some question Israel's right to exist at all. Conflict between Arabs and Jews is so deeply entangled with the geography and history of the region that it is difficult to envision how it can be put to rest, despite the desire of most on both sides. At its simplest, the extraordinarily complicated and frequently violent situation in which modern Israel finds itself is the result of two strong and passionate groups needing to live side by side but being unable to do so.

The conflict between Arabs and Jews, however, is only one of the dilemmas facing Israel today. Jews have radically different visions of the purpose of their homeland. Some think of Israel simply as the only place on earth where being Jewish is not unusual, while others see it in religious terms as the land promised to the Jews by God in return for following his laws. The conflicts between these two visions are central to many issues in Israel today. Underneath all the dilemmas, however, lies a unifying thread that has survived every controversy and every threat to the Jewish people: a belief in human brotherhood under the eye of an all-powerful God.

The Zionist Vision and the Arab Response

Until recent times, a loose sense of human brotherhood did exist between Arabs and Jews in the parched deserts and hills of Palestine. It was not until the growth of Zionism at the turn of the twentieth century that the political and sociological shifts that would spawn the current conflict began. The Zionists wanted the land they called Eretz Israel (the Land of Israel) to belong to the Jews alone. By the 1920s, hostility between the two groups over the right to the land had already begun to take lives. After World War II, the United Nations formally established a Jewish homeland in part of Palestine, but the Palestinian Arabs did not accept this. A bloody War of Independence over control of the region took place upon the declaration of the State of Israel in 1948.

During the conflict, thousands of Palestinians moved into refugee camps across the borders in the West Bank, then part of the nation of Transjordan, and in the Gaza Strip, which borders Egypt. Most thought this would be a temporary arrangement, that they would eventually resettle in neighboring Arab countries or return to their homes after the anticipated defeat of the Jews. But exile became permanent when the new Israeli nation defeated the Arab forces and the Palestinians found themselves inside the borders of an expanded Israel. They were not offered the chances they expected to resettle in large numbers in surrounding Arab countries or to return to their homes. As a result, many Palestinians have now lived for several generations in squalor in refugee camps and crowded border cities. Tragically, the violence of today was born from these conditions.

A Jewish Nation

The new nation of Israel was concerned with its own refugees. Survivors of the Holocaust of World War II, during which more than 6 million Jews were murdered simply for being Jewish, came in shiploads. Jews from Iraq, Yemen, and elsewhere were

Jewish and Arab activists call for an end to the fighting during a rally in Jerusalem in April 2002.

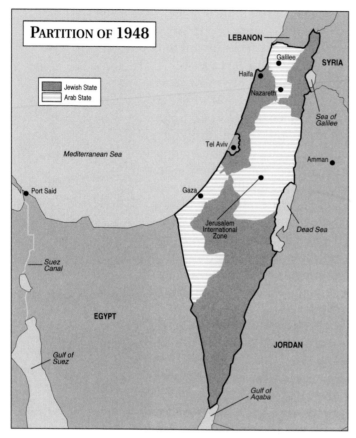

PARTITION OF 1948

Jewish State
Arab State

LEBANON

Galilee

SYRIA

Haifa

Nazareth

Sea of Galilee

Tel Aviv

Amman

Mediterranean Sea

Port Said

Gaza

Jerusalem International Zone

Dead Sea

Suez Canal

EGYPT

JORDAN

Gulf of Suez

Gulf of Aqaba

rescued in large numbers from hostile situations by airlifts and other means and brought to the new nation. They carried with them rich Jewish traditions unfamiliar to the Zionists, who had largely come from Europe. From the beginning, a new Israeli Jewish identity began to develop from the blended practices and customs of the Ashkenazic (European) and Sephardic (Middle Eastern and North African) groups. What appealed to both the Zionists and the Middle Eastern Jews was the idea of living without the persecution and the restrictions on their ability to practice their faith that had been the experience of Jews almost everywhere they had settled for nearly two thousand years.

At the core of the nation formed by this group of Jews of varying backgrounds is Jewish law. Although Israel has democratic institutions such as a representative government and elections, it is nevertheless a state where religious law, as interpreted by very strict Orthodox rabbis from biblical texts, takes precedence. Things falling under the umbrella of Jewish law are not put to a vote, ruled against in court, or subject to change other than by a rabbinical ruling. For example, even though roughly three-quarters of the Jews in Israel are secular, or nonreligious, only Orthodox rabbis can perform marriages, and they refuse to marry not only couples of different faiths but also couples who practice a form of Judaism other than Orthodoxy. Typically, secular and non-Orthodox Israelis shrug their shoulders about having to go to nearby Cyprus or elsewhere outside the country to marry. They also accept the difficulty of buying foods prohibited by Jewish kosher laws and the shutdown of public transportation on the Sabbath, saying that that is just the way things are in Israel. Although some Israelis feel that the rules are still not strict enough, and others are offended by any restrictions placed on them, most Israelis see the benefits of living in a place where Jewish ways dominate, even if they do sometimes seem a bit old-fashioned and out of touch.

"NEVER AGAIN"

Jews know all too well the price of being a minority. The horrors of the Holocaust are an inseparable part of Jewish identity today. The phrase "never again" is repeated often, referring to the passive and disbelieving way most Jews reacted to the Nazis. The Jewish way, as most Israelis view it, is nonviolent, but many now believe that the best defense is a good offense. Israeli Jews feel at the deepest level of their identity a commitment to the survival of what is to them their Promised Land. This commitment is reflected in the generally positive spirit with which they accept military service, which includes many years of reserve duty, during which they can be called away from their families and professional lives on a moment's notice. It is reflected in older Israelis' concerns that young people are tired of hearing about the Holocaust and the price that was paid in Jewish lives to establish their nation. It is reflected in their passionate disagreements about how to respond to Palestinian extremists who blow themselves up in crowds of Israelis. But it is also reflected in the beauty of Hebrew songs that float over the airwaves, many of which tell of the bittersweetness of life in a country where love must find a way to thrive despite violence. It is also reflected in enduring Jewish traditions such as the greeting offered as the sun sets each Friday, "Shabbat Shalom" ("Sabbath Peace"), even by those who have no intention of otherwise observing a peaceful day of rest.

ONE PEOPLE, ONE NATION

The profound level at which the people of Israel identify as Jews is perhaps best reflected in the lack of self-consciousness with which faith is expressed. *Kippot*, small skullcaps, adorn the heads of Israeli teens in blue jeans and T-shirts, dusty construction workers stopping for lunch at the local falafel stand,

A Bar-mitzvah rite takes place in front of Jerusalem's Wailing Wall.

little boys riding their bicycles, and men touching their lips to the graves of long-dead rabbis. The long, curled forelocks of Orthodox boys in dark coats bounce as they kick a ball in the park, while their bearded and identically dressed fathers converse and keep a watchful eye. Men and women bend and bob over prayer books on bus seats, in quiet corners of airports, and in shadowed alleys off bustling streets. Though many Israelis may grumble that such devotion to faith is excessive and, some say, even oppressive to the less observant, most seem to accept the fact that the strictly observant have, in a very real way, "kept the faith" so that all, even the less observant, can live as Jews today and in the future.

There is a sense of family among Israelis, a deep feeling of commonality of background and experience, regardless of whether the face belongs to a Yemenite Kurd, an Ethiopian, or a survivor of Auschwitz; whether it belongs to an ultra-Orthodox man under a white and blue prayer shawl or an elegant woman eating in the dining room of a five-star hotel. Though Israelis may be openly intolerant of each other's political perspectives or level of religious observance, arguing passionately as all families do, they still look each other in the eyes and see kinship. Whether they and their neighbors can do the same thing may be the question on which the global future will depend.

Ha'aretz:
The Land

To find Israel on a map, most people locate the eastern end of the Mediterranean Sea and point dead center. In truth, Israel is so small that if it were located elsewhere it might be difficult to find at all. Israel is a tiny country, slightly smaller than New Jersey. It constitutes less than 1 percent of the land of the Middle East. Even in its expanded size, which today includes the disputed territories of the West Bank, Golan Heights, and Gaza Strip, it is less than thirteen thousand square miles total—approximately three hundred miles from north to south and about sixty miles across. If, as many predict, Israel relinquishes much of its current territory to allow the creation of a Palestinian state, it will shrink to approximately two-thirds its current size, becoming one of the smallest nations on earth, in some places less than ten miles wide.

Jews from all over the world have brought their distinct cultures to the place they call simply Ha'aretz (the land). Arabs and Christians have also made their mark on a land characterized by biblical images of hostile deserts roamed by nomads, narrow green river deltas, and gleaming white stone cities. But Israel also has modern cities such as Haifa and Tel Aviv. It has large agricultural tracts of fruit trees and grains. It has swamps, forests, mountains, coral reefs, and even snow. This geographic variety makes Israel an endlessly fascinating place.

JERUSALEM

At the heart of Israel, both geographically and spiritually, is the city of Jerusalem. Today, Jerusalem is a hub of three faiths—Judaism, Christianity, and Islam. Jewish history in Jerusalem began with the City of David, a much-visited archaeological site dating from approximately 1000 B.C., located just outside the ancient city walls. The most sacred site

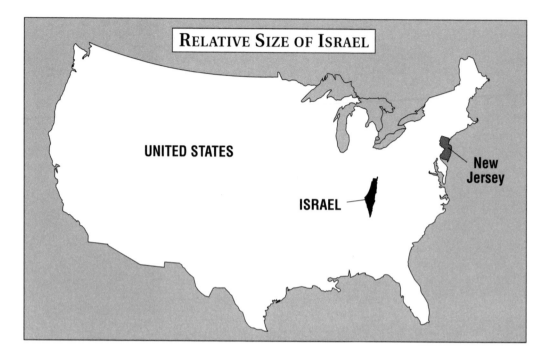

RELATIVE SIZE OF ISRAEL

UNITED STATES

New Jersey

ISRAEL

in Judaism is found in Jerusalem: the Western, or Wailing, Wall, inside the ancient wall of the Old City. It is the only surviving part of the Second Temple, which was the center of Jewish worship until its destruction by the Romans in the first century A.D.

The Western Wall is overlooked by Temple Mount, home to the beautiful and ornate Muslim shrine, the Dome of the Rock, said to be the place Muhammad ascended to heaven. Christians also revere Jerusalem, flocking there and nearby Bethlehem to visit sites associated with Jesus Christ, including the garden at Gethsemane, where he spent the last night of his life, and the traditionally accepted sites of his crucifixion and resurrection.

The Old City of Jerusalem is divided into Jewish, Armenian, Christian, and Muslim quarters, characterized by narrow streets and alleys opening onto small, sunny squares. Many of the main passageways are covered with awnings and lined with tourist shops and tiny cafés frequented by residents. Rimming the Old City are walls broken by gates that have served as the only entry points to the walled city since biblical times. Today, a walk atop the walls is a popular outing, providing a view of the entire city and its surroundings. In winter months, the view includes an occasional dusting of snow because of Jerusalem's location in the Judean Hills, the highest elevation in central Israel.

Outside the ancient walls, a contemporary city exists among the remnants of the past. The eastern section is part of the West Bank, which is Palestinian territory. It includes the Mount of Olives, which is said to have been frequented by Jesus, and Mount Scopus, the site of the world-renowned Hebrew University. The western section of Jerusalem is the heart of daily life for many city dwellers, and the center of the nation's government. Here can be found the huge and colorful vegetable market, Mahane Yehuda, and the center of government, the Knesset. Nearby are luxury hotels, modern office buildings, and the world-famous Israel Museum. The museum is home to, among many other priceless artifacts, the Dead Sea Scrolls, which are handwritten copies of biblical and other texts dating from the time of Jesus. Also in the west is Mount Herzl, a beautiful forest park containing the graves of fallen soldiers as well as many prime ministers, including Yitzhak Rabin and Golda Meir. Another much-visited site is Yad Vashem, the Holocaust museum and memorial garden.

THE OLD CITY OF JERUSALEM

Church of the Holy Sepulchre ●

Christian Quarter

Muslim Quarter

Dome of the Rock ●

Armenian Quarter ●

The Western Wall

El Aqsa Mosque ●

● Church of St. James

Jewish Quarter

☆ PLANTING TREES

According to *Insight Guide: Israel,* from the time of the first Zionist settlers in the late nineteenth century, "the act of planting a tree came to symbolize the redemption of the Jewish homeland." This campaign began in the Jezreel Valley in northern Israel when newly drained swampland was turned into fertile soil. Over the years, 125 million trees have been planted in the region, including a large forest named after Arthur Balfour, the British foreign minister who first proposed that Great Britain support a Jewish homeland in Israel. Today, visitors can continue the tradition at the many tree-planting centers there and throughout the country. Tree planting is so important in Israel that the Jewish holiday of Tu b'Shevat, which was the date set in biblical times for the determination of the tithe on the fruits from trees, has been revived as a holiday on which schoolchildren take field trips to plant trees all over the nation.

Among the greatest honors that can be given to a supporter of the Jews is to have a tree planted on the Avenue of the Righteous Gentiles in Yad Vashem. Located there are trees in honor of Raoul Wallenberg, a Swedish diplomat credited with saving thousands of Hungarian Jews before his disappearance into a prison camp in the Soviet Union; Oskar Schindler and his wife, Emilie, Germans who saved more than a thousand Jews during the Holocaust; and hundreds of others who acted courageously to save Jews during World War II.

Ironically, Jerusalem means "dwelling of peace." Today, as often in the past, that name has proven sadly inappropriate. The complexities of life in modern-day Israel are illustrated by Jerusalem. Both Palestinians and Israelis claim Jerusalem as their rightful capital, and its division today into Palestinian and Israeli sections has pleased almost no one. Passions run higher about Jerusalem than perhaps any other city in the world, and the issue of who will, and will not, control it has been the point on which many peace talks between Arabs and Israelis have broken down.

THE NORTH

North of Jerusalem lies the Jezreel Valley. It is a lush stretch of green known not only for its great agricultural productivity but also for its spiritual significance. Today, parts of the

valley lie in the West Bank. Located in the valley's Israeli parts
is the city of Jesus's childhood, Nazareth. Nazareth is home to
the largest church in the Middle East, the Basilica of the An-
nunciation, which commemorates where Mary is reputed to
have been told by the angel Gabriel that she was pregnant
with the son of God.

North of Nazareth is a mountainous area where one of the
most fascinating towns in Israel, Safed, is located. Safed is
home to a famous artists' colony, but it is best known as a
center of Jewish mysticism. Many Jewish scholars congre-
gated in Safed in the 1500s and developed the Kabbalah, the
most important Jewish mystical text. Today, Safed's cobble-
stoned streets are still filled with Orthodox men in black hats
and coats rushing to services at tiny but extravagantly deco-
rated synagogues dating back several centuries. And the
sounds of religious chanting spill from the windows and
doorways of religious centers known as yeshivas. Near Safed
is the town of Rosh Pinna, where one of the oldest Zionist settlements is now being painstakingly restored.

A finger of land leads north from Safed to the Hula Valley;
Mount Hermon, on the Lebanese and Syrian borders; and the
Golan Heights. The Hula Valley is one of the marvels of the
early Jewish state. Before 1950, it was "malaria-infested swamp
land—home to snakes, water buffalo and wild boar."[1] But by
1957 it had been drained and planted, and several settlements
had been established. Northeast is Mount Hermon, where Israeli skiers flock during winter months. Overlooking the Hula
Valley to the east is the Golan Heights, which is a source of
continuous strife with Syria, who claims the region as part of
its territory. Approximately thirteen thousand Israelis cur-
rently live in this region, known for its award-winning winer-
ies. This further complicates the relationship with Syria,
because it is clear from their development of the area that the
Israelis do not intend to leave. But, as travel author Pam Barrett describes, strife is not new to this region of "somber
[mountains] doomed by history and bloodied by almost
ceaseless war."[2] Its value as an overlook and a passageway
from the interior of the Middle East to the coastal plains of the
Mediterranean has made it a battleground for centuries.

One of the best-known landmarks of northern Israel is the
large freshwater lake known as the Sea of Galilee, which lies
southwest of the Golan Heights. Here, Jesus is said to have

walked on water, fed the masses on a few fish and loaves of bread, and preached the Sermon on the Mount. Here also is the Roman city of Tiberias, where Jewish scholars of later eras wrote the first commentary on the Bible, known as the Mishna. The great medieval scholar Moses Maimonides is buried here as well. Today, the Sea of Galilee is best known for its modern beach resorts where Israelis go to water ski, windsurf, sunbathe, and just relax in the many cafés and restaurants.

The Jordan River begins its path to the Dead Sea at the south end of the Sea of Galilee. Many Christians gather along the river at the spot where Jesus is said to have been baptized, but for most Israelis the location is more significant as the site of the founding of Deganya and Kinneret, the first two collective farming villages known as kibbutzim (the plural of kibbutz). Still in existence today, kibbutzniks, as their members are called, work as part of a community, sharing both labor and profit and making decisions as a group. Just south of these towns are the famous Roman ruins at Bet She'an, bordering the West Bank.

Jenin and Nablus are two of the major cities in the hot and dry West Bank portion of this region. The West Bank stretches so far west at this point that Israel is at its narrowest, about fifteen minutes across by car. The location of Jenin in particular has made it a center of anti-Israeli operations, because a terrorist can be across the border and in Haifa, Netanya, or another coastal city in less than half an hour.

A depiction of the baptism of Jesus on the Jordan River.

THE DEAD SEA

By far the most recognizable feature of the Judean Desert is the Dead Sea. It and the Jordan River, which feeds it from the north, form the country's eastern border. About half of the western side of the Dead Sea would remain part of Israel if the West Bank became part of a sovereign Palestine. This half contains the resorts of Ein Gedi and Ein Bokek as well as the Dead Sea Mineral Works, where blowing salt conveys a seemingly perpetual snowstorm in the desert heat.

The Dead Sea, thirteen hundred feet below sea level, creates an eerie landscape. Large clumps of salt crystals float on its surface, and its colors change as the sun and clouds pass across the sky. The Dead Sea has shrunk in recent years as a result of the diversion of water from the Jordan River for irrigation in the north. The sea has no outlet, so all the minerals leeched from the surrounding cliffs by erosion remain in its water and become concentrated through evaporation. The intensely salty water prohibits animal life, hence the English name Dead Sea; the sea is known as Yam Melach, or Salt Sea, in Hebrew. The concentration of salt in the water provides swimmers with the entertaining experience of bobbing on top of the water high enough to read a book without having to use a raft. Expensive resort hotels and spas line the Israeli shoreline, but many people stay in the numerous campsites and inexpensive kibbutzim nearby and provide their own spa experience by wading in the water and rubbing what is considered to be the therapeutic (and expensive) Dead Sea mud all over themselves free of charge.

A sign posted near the Dead Sea, written in Hebrew, Arabic, and English.

THE COAST

This vulnerable northern stretch of Israel's coast, approaching the border with Lebanon, is a region of resort communities scattered among beaches and surf-pounded cliffs. Haifa, the biggest northern city, is an important port and the center of Israel's high-tech and petrochemical industries. Though it has been a port since ancient times, Haifa is thoroughly modern. It is home to one of the major Arab populations and

yet another faith centered in Israel, the Baha'i. The gold
dome of the Baha'i Shrine of the Bab is the most noticeable
landmark in the city.

South of Haifa is the Plain of Sharon, another region of re-
claimed swampland now dominated by citrus crops. Located
in the region are a famous nature reserve, the Mount Carmel
National Park, and one of the most important archaeological
sites in Israel, the ancient seaside city of Caesarea. Caesarea
(named after Roman emperor Caesar Augustus) was one of
the prizes captured by the Christians in 1101, during the First
Crusade. Visitors can stroll among the ruins of the crusaders'
homes and see the remnants of Roman buildings jutting out
above the gentle surf.

TEL AVIV

Right in the middle of the Mediterranean coast of Israel lies
the city of Tel Aviv. While Jerusalem is the spiritual, historical,
and political capital of Israel, Tel Aviv is unquestionably its
economic and entertainment center. Though Tel Aviv itself
has only 350,000 residents, the surrounding suburbs swell
the population to over 2 million, one-third of the nation's total. Tel Aviv is one of the few cities in Israel with no ancient
base. It was first intended in the early twentieth century to
house the overflow population from adjoining Jaffa, but
quickly the roles became reversed. Tel Aviv grew without any
planned architectural style and still retains a chaotic feel today, complete with congested freeways, chic shopping
streets, high-rise apartments, and tattered and neglected
housing for the poor.

Tel Aviv is the most exciting city in Israel. Nightlife
abounds along the beaches and main thoroughfares such as
Dizengoff Street, especially in the summer, when the oppressive daytime heat and humidity (characteristic of all but
the highest elevations of Israel) make the cool of evening a
pleasant release. The world-class Israeli symphony has its
home in Tel Aviv, as does the New Israel Opera and world-
renowned Tel Aviv University.

Though Tel Aviv is thoroughly modern, its ethnic roots are
still central to its overall identity. The Yemenite Quarter is "a
jolt back in time,"[3] and various open markets, or *shouks*, such
as the Carmel Market, are dazzling kaleidoscopes of colorful
clothing and other merchandise, with the pungent smells of

spices and cooking meat and music blaring from competing boom boxes. The city of Jaffa, immediately to the south, has one of the longest histories in Israel. There was already an important port on this spot at the time of Solomon, approximately one millennium B.C. Portions of the old city were recently saved from demolition and restored as an artists' colony and tourist attraction.

FROM THE JUDEAN DESERT TO THE RED SEA

Less than two hours by car from bustling Tel Aviv and only a few minutes east of Jerusalem and the suburb of Bethlehem lies the Judean Desert. Here, Bedouin shepherds in traditional headdresses still tend flocks and people still go from place to place on donkeys and flatbed trucks. Small Arab villages and Jewish settlements dot the landscape, along with the famed biblical cities of Jericho and Hebron, today both in the West Bank. Streambeds called wadis lie dry and bare, while above them rise cliffs pocked with caves that, over the centuries, have been used as places for spiritual retreats and hiding places for revolutionaries. On top of one of these cliffs

The modern city of Tel Aviv meets the Mediterranean Sea just north of the historic city of Jaffa.

lie the ruins of the Roman ruler Herod's fortress at Masada, where a group of Jews during the Roman revolt around A.D. 70 chose to commit mass suicide rather than be captured and enslaved by the Roman Legion.

Masada overlooks the Dead Sea, the central landmark of the Judean Desert, and the mountains of Jordan on its far side. South of the Dead Sea, the panorama of the Negev and Arava Deserts unfolds. Sunlight and the mineral composition of the rocks and mountains create ever-changing colors, and in places, it looks as desolate as the surface of the moon. Although the region contains Israel's fourth largest city, Beersheba, and one of its major universities, Ben-Gurion University, the Negev is best known for these lonely and spectacular desert landscapes, as well as the numerous Bedouin camps that dot its plains.

The Negev is shaped like a dagger. Its western edge is the Sinai Peninsula, part of Egypt, and its eastern edge is Jordan.

The waters of the Red Sea offer a dizzying array of coral and tropical fish.

The adjacent Arava Desert contains the ruins of King Solomon's Mines, a remarkable copper-mining and smelting facility dating from biblical times. The dagger comes to a tip in Elat, a resort and port at the top of the Red Sea. The Red Sea, which derives its name from the biblical Sea of Reeds, is a major destination for underwater enthusiasts; it is said to have more species of fish among its spectacular coral reefs than any other body of water in the world.

Elat is sometimes called Israel's first city, because it was where the Hebrews, led by Moses, are thought to have first set foot on what eventually became Israel. Here, as in so many places in Israel, the old and new merge. Here also, the shadowy hills of Jordan, Saudi Arabia, and Egypt in the distance place Israel in the larger context of the Middle East. They serve as reminders that Israel has done a better job mastering the natural environment than the political one and that, despite its long heritage and recent achievements, it is still a very fragile and vulnerable place.

2

A Vision in the Desert: The Creation of a Jewish Homeland

The first five books of the Bible, known to Jews as the Torah, contain some of the most famous stories ever told. In one, Jacob wrestles all night with an angel, who in the morning rewards his struggle by renaming him Israel, "he who struggles." Generations later, God parts the Red Sea, drowning the pharaoh's army and bringing the children of Israel, as the Hebrews called themselves, to freedom. After receiving the stone tablets of the Ten Commandments, Moses leads his people to the Promised Land. There, years later, David kills Goliath and becomes king. His successor, King Solomon, builds a great temple in Jerusalem and rules with such intelligence that his name becomes synonymous with wisdom.

To Jews, these are far more than exciting stories. They are their personal heritage, almost as if each is a family legend about their own great grandparents. A feeling of deep connection to their ancient history is one of the things that connects Jews not only to their past but to each other in the present. Their history also conveys to them a sense of special destiny. They believe that their ancestors entered into a covenant with God that obligated them to follow laws such as the Ten Commandments in return for God's protection and His promise to guide the children of Israel to their homeland and sustain them there.

Through the millennia since that time, Jews have viewed this "Promised Land" as a primary symbol of God's will for them. This deep-seated belief is essential to understanding how the modern nation of Israel came into existence and continues to survive. It also plays a role in the reasons behind Israel's decisions, attitudes, and actions today, and the challenges it faces in the future.

THE JEWISH DIASPORA

Several centuries after the last events of the Old Testament, and a few decades after the crucifixion of Jesus Christ, another momentous event took place in Jewish history. Around A.D. 135, after a failed revolt against Roman rule, the Jews were forced to leave their homeland, an event known as the Jewish Diaspora. Though some Jews stayed behind, as much as 90 percent of the population began what would amount to nearly two thousand years of exile. Over the centuries, Jews moved across the globe, settling in as a minority in countries on five continents. Because they continued to follow Jewish laws regarding what they ate, what they wore, how and when they worshiped, and who they would and would not marry, they tended to stick out wherever they went. And because

This nineteenth-century painting shows Moses (background) leading the Israelites out of Egypt and into the Promised Land.

their different practices often made interaction difficult, Jews often did not object to being isolated in their own neighborhoods.

As a result, Jews often became the targets of suspicion whenever there was a problem in the larger community. Anything bad was blamed on them, from natural phenomena such as earthquakes and plagues, to political and economic instability in a country, to personal misfortunes such as the death of a child. The irrationality of such anti-Semitic claims only made them more dangerous because there was nothing Jews could do to counter with reason or logic a hatred that often boiled over into open persecution and violence.

THEODOR HERZL AND THE BIRTH OF ZIONISM

In the late nineteenth century, a particularly savage series of anti-Semitic events known as pogroms occurred in eastern Europe. Whole communities of Jews were slaughtered and their synagogues and homes destroyed. As a result, many Jewish families decided to immigrate to western Europe, where they thought they might find a more tolerant environment.

A young Jewish journalist named Theodor Herzl had immigrated with his family to Vienna to escape pogroms in Hungary. In 1895, while working in Paris as his Viennese newspaper's French correspondent, Herzl covered the treason trial of a Jewish army officer, Alfred Dreyfus. Despite clear evidence pointing to another non-Jewish officer, Dreyfus was convicted. Herzl attended a public ceremony in which Dreyfus was stripped of his medals and insignias before being sent to Devil's Island, a hard-labor camp off the coast of South America. During this public shaming, the crowd chanted "Death to the Jews."

At that moment, standing in a Paris street, Herzl realized that as long as Jews remained a minority, there would be no safe place for them. Herzl became singularly focused on this revelation and published a book, *The Jewish State*, a year later. The book advocated the idea of establishing a Jewish homeland where Jews could live according to the dictates of their faith, building by their own hard work a better, more dignified, and safer life. Many Jews quickly embraced this idea, named Zionism after Mount Zion in Jerusalem. In 1897, the first Zionist conference was held in Switzerland, resulting

THEODOR HERZL

Theodor Herzl was an unlikely candidate to become the catalyst of the Zionist movement. The son of Hungarian Jews who had settled in Vienna to escape the pogroms, he grew up with no particularly strong identification with being Jewish. For the Herzls, as for many European Jews living sophisticated city lives, assimilation was the goal. They strove to be as much like their neighbors as possible and downplayed their Jewishness. Theodor, known for his dapper style of dress and refined tastes, wrote poetry and plays and saw himself as a well-educated, middle-class man, no different from his Christian peers.

After the Dreyfus trial awakened him to the deeply rooted anti-Semitism in European society, Herzl became obsessed with the idea of establishing a safe haven for Jews somewhere in the world. He published a book called *The Jewish State* in 1896, in which he outlined the need for a Jewish homeland and his ideas about how it would be developed and organized. Herzl was not overly concerned with where the Jewish homeland would be, even expressing interest in Great Britain's offer of land in its colony in Uganda or perhaps in Canada. But he recognized that, for his supporters, the emotional pull of the "Promised Land" was part of the appeal of Zionism. He spent the rest of his life trying to get support for Zionism, writing essays, speeches, and even a visionary novel, *Old-New Land*, which describes Palestine before and after the establishment of a Jewish state.

Herzl was not actually the first person to promote the idea of Zionism. Moses Hess developed the idea in the 1860s and Leon Pinsker built on it in the 1880s. Though Herzl was only modestly successful at moving concrete plans for a Jewish state forward before his premature death from pneumonia at age forty-four, his name has become synonymous with the dream of a nation of Israel. Today, his burial place, one of the most beautiful parts of Jerusalem, is named Mount Herzl in his memory.

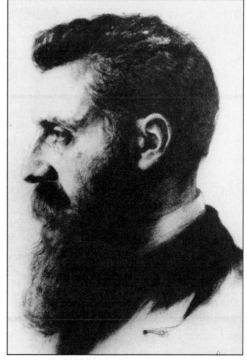

Theodor Herzl, founder of the World Zionist Organization.

in the formation of the World Zionist Organization. With Herzl as chairman, the World Zionist Organization began to coordinate efforts to make the dream of a Jewish homeland a reality. At the fifth conference in 1901, the Jewish National Fund was set up to buy land and finance the relocation and expenses of Jews willing to settle in Palestine, as the area of today's Israel was then called. By 1909, the organization's efforts resulted in the establishment of Tel Aviv, a new city created as the first all-Jewish city in the world, and the first kibbutz at Deganya.

UNDERCURRENTS OF CONTROVERSY

Many Arabs living in Palestine initially welcomed the small numbers of Zionists because they thought their skills, knowledge, and enthusiasm would bring advancements that would benefit everyone. However, as the numbers of Zionists grew, the Arabs became alarmed. It was not Jews they objected to,

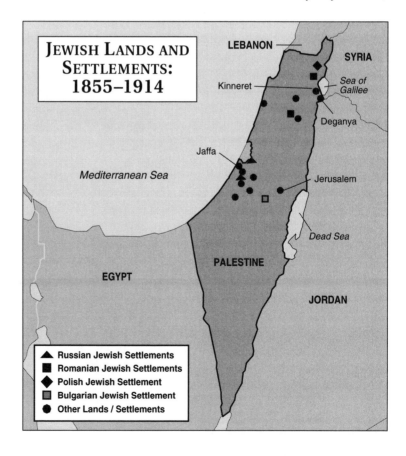

Palestinian Arabs said, but Zionists. Nothing about the religions themselves made coexistence difficult. But when Zionists began to purchase land and force off Arabs who had lived there for centuries, it was clear that they wanted not to coexist but to claim the whole region for themselves. Scholar Benny Morris summarizes the two groups' conflicting goals: "The Arabs sought instinctively to retain the Arab and Muslim character of the region and to maintain their position as its rightful inhabitants; the Zionists sought radically to change the status quo, buy as much land as possible, settle on it, and eventually turn an Arab-populated country into a Jewish homeland."[4]

The situation between the Arabs and the Jews was not the only one that was deteriorating in the region. During the First World War (1914–1918), the Turkish-based Ottoman Empire, which controlled Palestine, allied itself with the Germans against Great Britain. When the British invaded Palestine in 1917 to protect their military and economic interests there, they found both the Arabs and the Jews more than willing to help them throw out the Ottoman Turks. The Arabs wanted to help the British because the British told the Arab leaders that, in exchange for their support in defeating the Turks, Palestine would become an independent nation. The Arabs interpreted this to mean that the British would support an Arab state in Palestine. However, the Jews also believed they had been promised Palestine. In late 1917, under the influence of Chaim Weizmann, a Zionist who would become the first president of Israel, the British had adopted the Balfour Declaration. Named for Foreign Secretary Arthur Balfour, its author and advocate, the declaration reassured the Jews of British support for "the establishment in Palestine of a national home for the Jewish people."[5]

THE BRITISH MANDATE

After the fall of the Ottoman Empire at the end of the war, the League of Nations (the precursor to today's United Nations) gave Great Britain a mandate over Palestine that made it the official governing body of the region while the future independent state took shape. Both Arabs and Zionist Jews welcomed the mandate because they believed they could use the power of the British authorities to advance their respective visions. From the beginning, however, some people on both

sides were concerned that the British mandate was headed
for disaster. Though their reasons varied, in general the concern was that it was impossible for both Arabs and Zionists
to get what they wanted because they both wanted the same
thing: an independent homeland on the same patch of land.
A letter handed to the British administration after a Jewish
"Balfour Day" celebration in Jerusalem in 1918 describes the
issue from the Arab point of view: "We have noticed yesterday

ELIEZER BEN-YEHUDA AND THE REVIVAL OF HEBREW

Raymond P. Scheindlin, in *A Short History of the Jewish People*,
states that "the most remarkable collective achievement of the
Jewish people in modern times, perhaps even more remarkable than the establishment of the State of Israel itself, has
been the revival of Hebrew." Eliezer Ben-Yehuda is the man
credited with that accomplishment. In 1881, well before the
Zionist movement was formally established, Ben-Yehuda
moved with his wife to Jerusalem. When their child was born,
he decided to try an experiment to see whether Hebrew was
still usable as a spoken language. (Hebrew had not been a spoken language since ancient times and had survived only
through written texts such as the Torah.) He forbade any com-
munication at all with his child except in Hebrew, even by
guests. When the child grew up to be fully capable of expressing whatever he wished in Hebrew, Ben-Yehuda proved that
Hebrew could be sufficient language for an entire nation.

Because Jews came from many countries and had no other
language in common (most Jews had at least some familiarity
with Hebrew from their religious education), Ben-Yehuda's
success with his child clearly played an important role for the
future nation. A Hebrew Language Committee was established
to create vocabulary words for things that did not exist in biblical times. Scholars and linguists did this by poring over ancient literature in Hebrew for words that could serve as roots,
then creating a new word from them.

Today, a century later, as children chatter in Hebrew in
school yards, Knesset members argue in Hebrew over the budget, someone buys a Hebrew newspaper from a street vendor,
and someone else scratches down a telephone message in Hebrew, Eliezer Ben-Yehuda's vision continues to be honored
and treasured.

a large crowd of Jews carrying banners and over-running the streets shouting words which hurt the feelings and wound the soul. They pretend with open voice that Palestine . . . which has been inhabited by the Arabs for long ages, who loved it and died defending it, is now a national home for them."[6]

Already, the extreme conflicting visions were taking shape. One Muslim group as early as 1919 used stark language to describe the perceived end result: "We will push the Zionists into the sea—or they will send us back into the desert."[7] Jewish leader David Ben-Gurion echoed these sentiments in the same year: "There is . . . no solution! There is a gulf and nothing can bridge it. We as a nation want this country to be *ours;* the Arabs, as a nation, want it to be *theirs.*"[8] British critics of the mandate argued that their regional interests could be adequately defended by other means, and the prestige associated with being responsible for the Holy Land was not worth the headaches already being caused by its quarreling inhabitants.

From the beginning, the British failed to take seriously enough the basic incompatibility of Arab and Zionist visions for the region, a fact that would have tragic and far-reaching consequences. The British seemed more concerned with establishing an outpost for their way of life—tennis, afternoon tea, flower gardens, military parades, and parties—than in addressing the problem of the growing tension between Arabs and Jews. During the three decades of the mandate, the British seemed to have no vision of what they wished to accomplish, no consistent policy toward either group, and no idea of how to fashion an effective compromise. Instead, they simply tried to appease both sides, while privately considering the situation unsolvable. The mandate was temporary, after all, and to many British, what happened to the region after they left was not their concern.

Both Arabs and Jews thought the British favored the other group, and examples of favoritism did abound on both sides throughout the mandate, creating a kind of balancing act that satisfied no one. One particularly devastating action for the Jews was the White Paper in 1939, which, despite impassioned protests by the Jews, prescribed severe limitations on Jewish immigration to Palestine just as the Nazis were coming to power in Germany. The White Paper was meant to reassure Arabs that Jews would not achieve a numerical majority in Palestine. The British also tried to soft-pedal the Balfour

THE HOLOCAUST AND THE ESTABLISHMENT OF ISRAEL

One-third of the world's Jews, and 70 percent of the Jews of Europe—more than 6 million people total, including 1.5 million children—died during World War II in a systematic attempt by the Nazis to destroy the Jews. Many people believe that the State of Israel was the brainchild of the victorious countries in that war, which wanted to give the Jews something in compensation for the Holocaust. This, however, is not an accurate picture of the founding of Israel.

Zionist Jews had been returning to their ancestral land to settle for half a century before the Holocaust. By the 1920s, there were 170,000 Jews in Palestine, and by the eve of World War II, their numbers had risen to 350,000. The idea of a formally designated Jewish homeland was internationally introduced by the British in the Balfour Declaration in 1917, long before World War II, and Zionists had worked diligently in Palestine for decades to develop an economy that could sustain any number of Jews who wished to resettle there.

In fact, immediately before and during World War II, the British put stringent limits on how many Jews could come to Palestine as a way of appeasing the Arabs who did not want Jews to become a majority. This policy directly contributed to the deaths of many Jews who tried to escape the reach of the Nazis but were unable to make it to safety in Palestine. After the war ended, despite knowledge of the extent of the Nazis' crimes against the Jews, the British blockaded Palestinian ports to keep refugee ships from landing. And rather than antagonize the Arabs by letting large numbers of Jews enter Palestine, they interned thousands of Jews recently released from concentration camps in squalid refugee camps in Cyprus. Then, despite the political chaos and violence that was certain to ensue, neither the United Nations nor the British made any effort to help the badly outnumbered Jews prepare to defend their territory when the British mandate ended.

For these reasons, Israelis today reject the notion that their homeland was in any sense the apologetic gift of a sensitive world. They believe that with their blood, sweat, and passionate vision, and often despite the actions of the rest of the world, they won it for themselves.

Declaration to the Arabs, saying that a Jewish state would take many generations to achieve and would not be permitted to undercut the rights of the Arabs in Palestine. However, this did little to stop the mistrust growing on both sides.

The British turned many Jews away who wanted to immigrate to Palestine, but they did little to slow the Jews down in their efforts to build a modern, economically sound society. Jews developed industries to harvest minerals from the Dead Sea; built new communities and transportation systems; and planted orchards, vineyards, and fields in newly irrigated deserts. This only served to antagonize the Arabs, who saw permanent buildings and newly tilled fields as evidence that the Zionists had, in effect, already won the battle for a homeland. Despite British efforts to play both sides, the Jews' sense of entitlement to keep Palestine for themselves grew with each acre they cultivated and each community they built. The growing economic disparity between the Arabs and the Jews was symbolic to both sides; the Jews felt it proved their earned title to the land, while the Arabs believed it illustrated their systematic and deliberate displacement from it.

THE END OF THE BRITISH MANDATE

The antagonism between the Arabs and Jews had escalated quickly after World War I. "[Arab] demonstrations, shop closures, petitions and placards reading 'Down with Zionism'" soon escalated into violence amid chants of "Palestine is our land and the Jews are our dogs" and "Kill the Jews."[9] In 1920, a riot broke out in Jerusalem that killed or wounded more than two hundred Jews and approximately thirty Arabs. The following year, Arabs rampaged through Jaffa, a town of twenty-six thousand Arabs and sixteen thousand Jews. Assisted by participating Arab police officers, Arabs looted and damaged Jewish property and "shot, stabbed and bludgeoned"[10] approximately forty newly arrived immigrant Jews. The following day, rioters in an orange grove on the outskirts of town murdered six more Jews, and by the end of the Jaffa riot, many Arabs had been killed as well. Though violence had occurred periodically before this, the Jerusalem and Jaffa riots marked a turning point that began to characterize the relationship between Arabs and Jews.

In 1936, the Arabs channeled their resentment of the perceived British favoritism of the Jews into what became known as the Palestinian Revolt. According to historian Benny Morris, "It was to be the biggest and most protracted uprising against the British in any country in the Middle East, and the most significant in Palestinian history until the anti-Israeli Intifada fifty years later."[11] It began with an Arab road ambush in which two Jews were killed, and escalated when the Jews retaliated by beating several Arabs. From that point forward, rumors of more murders and violence flew on both sides, and Arabs and Jews began striking back, sometimes in retaliation for things that had not actually occurred. Once peace was restored, Arab strikes brought the country to an economic stop. Railroads, highways, oil pipelines, tele-

A riot ensues in the city of Jaffa, in 1938.

✡ THE MUFTI OF JERUSALEM

Haj Amin al-Husseini (1893–1974) served as mufti, the Muslim spiritual leader of Jerusalem, from 1921 to 1936, and was the most powerful Arab in Palestine during the British mandate. Among al-Husseini's accomplishments as mufti was the restoration of the Dome of the Rock, including regilding its famous dome. This and the restoration of the nearby Al-Aqsa Mosque enhanced not only Jerusalem's prestige in the Muslim world but also his own.

However, it is his singular focus on defeating the Zionists and the British for which al-Husseini is best known. After the Jerusalem riots in 1920, he was sentenced to ten years in prison for his role in inciting violence, but he escaped across the border into the country of Transjordan. He returned in less than a year amid a storm of controversy. Al-Husseini had apparently taken steps to quell further violence after the riots and thus had earned new British high commissioner Herbert Samuel's wary approval. Samuel offered him amnesty and the appointment as mufti in exchange for al-Husseini's promise to work with Samuel, a Jew, to keep peace in the region. A year later, Samuel appointed al-Husseini head of the Supreme Muslim Council, another prestigious post. Though the Jews roundly criticized Samuel's actions as traitorous, he felt that it was better to try to work with al-Husseini than have him actively plotting against the Jews and the British.

Samuel's decision, however, turned out to be a grave error. Al-Husseini worked devotedly behind the scenes to foment Arab hatred against Jews and encouraged ongoing violence against them. The mufti was too powerful by then to unseat. He stayed in power until 1936, when he was finally removed from the post for his role in riots in 1929 and 1936. Al-Husseini then left Palestine and spent the rest of his life acting out his hatred against the British and the Jews by rallying Muslims in a variety of causes against both groups. Most notably, he openly allied himself with Hitler during World War II and participated in extermination efforts against the Jews in Bosnia, Hungary, and elsewhere. Militant Muslims see the mufti as a great leader and hero today.

Muslim Haj Amin Al-Husseini served as mufti of Jerusalem from 1921 to 1936.

phone lines, and government property were sabotaged. A group known as the Arab High Committee, ruled by the grand mufti of Jerusalem, the highest-ranking Muslim in Palestine, coordinated the revolt. According to author Daniel Jacobs, "At the height of the revolt, the rebels ran most of the country, with their own courts and taxes, and British rule

[was] more fiction than reality."[12] It took twenty-thousand British troops to regain control of Palestine. The mufti slipped over the border to Lebanon, where he continued to agitate against the British and the Jews.

During the remaining years of the British mandate, violent conflict became a part of life. Underground militias such as the Jewish Haganah and fringe groups such as Irgun and the Stern Gang plotted acts of sabotage against Arabs, and Arabs did the same to the Jews. As the British switched alliances on what seemed almost a daily basis in the mid-1940s, both sides began committing acts of violence against them as well, including a 1946 explosion by the Haganah at the King David Hotel in Jerusalem, which was the British administrative headquarters and a favorite spot for social gatherings.

Not too long after this demoralizing event, which killed ninety-one people, the British decided they had had enough. They announced their intention to leave Palestine the following year, leaving the United Nations in charge of finding a solution to the escalating violence. The United Nations responded in November 1947 with Resolution 181, which divided Palestine into separate Jewish and Arab regions. It was a bitterly contested decision that, rather than calming the situation, enraged the Arabs. As they had long feared, they found themselves stripped of land, now officially handed by the United Nations to the Jews.

The British had spent untold monetary and human resources on a project they thought would enhance their regional security and international prestige. It had done neither. If they had used the power of their mandate to help Arabs and Jews find a way to live side by side in Palestine, subsequent history might have been quite different. But as it was, even as the British packed their bags, the Arabs and the Zionists were stockpiling weapons and making plans to go to war.

Promises to Keep: Building a Jewish Nation

Although the United Nations had hoped that separate Jewish and Arab territories in Palestine would be a solution to the violence, the idea had become instead a new source of conflict. The Jews accepted partition because for the first time in nearly two millennia they would have a homeland, however small. The Arabs, on the other hand, were determined to undo the partition after the British left by retaking all of Palestine. During the six months between the official partition and the British withdrawal, Jews and Arabs continued a nearly constant campaign of sabotage and terrorism, a bloody undertaking that took two thousand lives between November 1947 and January 1948 alone.

While the British took erratic and inconsistent steps to intervene, Arabs and Jews fought for the positions they knew they would need for defense or attack when the British withdrew. Villages were attacked, vehicles were ambushed, and public places were shattered by bombings. In the earliest stages, Arabs were the major aggressors, but as time passed, the Jews began their own campaigns in retaliation, and before long both sides had staggering grief and pain to point to as they continued the escalating cycle of revenge.

The War of Independence

Both sides also used the last few months of the mandate to get ready for a war that would decide whether an independent Jewish nation would indeed take root in the Middle East. The Jews were badly outnumbered, representing only 30 percent of the population of Palestine, and were surrounded by four Arab nations. However, they improved their odds by thorough planning and strong organization.

By the time David Ben-Gurion proclaimed the "self-evident right of the Jewish people to be a nation" and "the establishment of the Jewish State in Palestine, to be called Israel, in the Declaration of Independence"[13] on May 14, 1948, the day before the end of the British mandate, Israel had a multiphased plan for its defense in place and an administrative structure to run the government and coordinate the war. Using a network of informants to obtain the schedule for British withdrawal, the newly declared Israelis were literally standing at the gates of British facilities, ready to occupy them the minute the British departed. The Haganah had been turned into a generally well-disciplined army of approximately sixty-five thousand regulars and reserves, and fringe elements who had been mounting raids on their own had largely been brought under Haganah control. Jewish agents were also scouring Europe for needed weapons, military vehicles, and ammunition.

David Ben-Gurion (center) announces the establishment of the state of Israel in 1948.

The Palestinian Arabs were also planning for war, but because of rivalries between Arab factions, particularly between the mufti and Fawzi al-Kaukji, another powerful Arab

leader in the region, these efforts were not well coordinated. No one in the mufti's faction had thought through the complexities of governing after the British left; instead, he had a nearly singular focus on forcing out the Jews and remaining the undisputed leader of the region. Factions continued to jockey for power among themselves rather than unite for a common purpose.

The larger Arab world claimed to support the Palestinians, but in fact was riddled with the same conflicts. Syria and Lebanon seemed more excited about the possibility of grabbing pieces of Palestine for themselves than helping the Palestinian Arabs in a unified fight against the Jews. Egypt was lukewarm about the war against the Jews, refusing to send armies until after the British left, and then not sending many troops at all. King Abdullah of Transjordan was supposedly in charge of a united Arab assault on Israel, but in fact he too hoped to gain as much of Palestine as possible for his own kingdom. According to historian Avi Shlaim, "The inability of the Arabs to coordinate their diplomatic and military plans was in no small measure responsible for the disaster that overwhelmed them."[14]

Though hostilities had been going on for years, the actual War of Independence took only a few months. The Israelis conquered almost 80 percent of the land that had been allocated to the Palestinians under the UN partition, fighting off largely ineffective invasions by Egypt, Transjordan, Iraq, and Syria. The West Bank and the Old City of Jerusalem were put under the control of Transjordan as part of a peace treaty with the new nation of Israel. Egypt took control of the Gaza Strip, a small region between Egypt and Israel on the Mediterranean Sea. The armistice that ended the War of Independence established what would be the new borders between Israel, Transjordan, and Egypt. This delineation, based on the land Israel controlled at the end of the fighting, became known as the Green Line. The Palestinians had lost everything the UN had allotted them, either to Israel or to their Arab neighbors, and they now found themselves without a home at all.

Homeless and Stateless

Suddenly outsiders in their own land, some Arabs left Israel by choice because they feared being the target of Jewish violence. Some left for other countries in the Middle East and around the world. Others simply moved east of the Green Line and settled in for what they thought would be a short stay in refugee camps. While some chose to leave, others left by at least some degree of force. Today, the question of how much was choice and how much was force is still hotly disputed. But regardless of the reason, the net effect was the same. According to historian Raymond P. Scheindlin, "Arab leaders reassured the

---

✡ THE SIEGE OF JERUSALEM

Before the end of the British mandate, both Arabs and Jews saw that the key to the Jews' ability to maintain a community in Jerusalem was to keep open the road serving as a supply corridor between Tel Aviv and Jerusalem. Without this, Jerusalem would be effectively under siege and would starve. The road starts on a coastal plain but soon begins an ascent several thousand feet to Jerusalem, winding through ravines with many Arab villages perched above. From these villages, raiders would wait for supply convoys, then swoop down, disable the vehicles, steal or destroy the supplies, and often murder the people. These raids were increasingly successful, and it became apparent that the villages would have to be neutralized to protect the convoys.

The most famous battle for control of the supply corridor took place at the Arab village of Kastel, just west of Jerusalem. There, over a period of several days in April 1948, a small group of Haganah soldiers, including a young officer named Yitzhak Rabin, who would later become prime minister, were able to capture the village and hold out against a more numerous but disorganized Arab force led by a popular community leader. Ironically, near-certain defeat for the Jewish forces was averted when they shot and killed this leader without even knowing who he was. When the death was discovered, all the Arabs in the village left for his funeral, giving Jewish reinforcements time to

arrive. With firm control of Kastel, the tide turned for control of the road, and Jerusalem, though it remained the scene of much violence, was not threatened by a siege again. Today, some of the ruins of the village of Kastel and the bunkers erected by the Haganah are preserved as a national monument.

An Israeli soldier stands guard over Arab prisoners in 1948.

refugees that the Arab countries would regroup, return to the battle, and restore them to their land of origin; the refugees were not absorbed into the other Arab countries, but were placed in camps, which turned into permanent abodes of poverty and despair, and where generations of refugees and their descendants nursed their hatred for Israel."[15]

Victors in what they considered a righteous and inevitable victory to secure their Promised Land, Israelis took steps to ensure that the refugees' move would be permanent. Several hundred Arab villages were destroyed. In 1950, the new government, led by David Ben-Gurion, the first prime minister of Israel, passed the Absentee Property Act, which stated that the property of anyone who had left during the war belonged to the state. Israeli citizens actually had legal title to only about 7 percent of the land their country controlled at the end of the war, but this act gave the nation title to the rest. The Law of Return, also passed in 1950, granted automatic Israeli citizenship to any Jew who came to live in Israel, and Jews from many parts of the world began arriving in large numbers. The new immigrants often took away jobs from those Arabs who had stayed behind, and the population boom prompted Israelis to create new communities in their expanded territory, a clear sign that they saw the land as permanently theirs. Both of these developments further soured the Arabs toward the Israelis.

WAR AND PEACE IN THE 1950S AND 1960S
During the first few years of its existence, Israel turned its attention to the many political, economic, and social challenges that were part of creating a nation that could feed, house, educate, and govern its people. The Israelis established the needed bureaucracy, passed laws, built roads and housing, opened schools and synagogues, developed businesses and industries, established hospitals and clinics, and expanded agricultural land. Though not unaware that their existence was still a source of anger and shame among the defeated Arabs, and a cause of suffering for the refugees, they did not see Israeli–Arab relations as a top priority.

In 1956, however, Israel's attention focused on its relationship with Egypt as a result of Egyptian president Gamal Abdel Nasser's declaration that the Suez Canal was no longer international property but belonged to and would be

Haganah soldiers in action on the border of Jaffa and Tel Aviv in 1949.

controlled exclusively by Egypt. Israel recognized that its use of the canal could be cut off, so it quickly moved, in concert with France and Great Britain, to retake the canal and reinstate it as an international zone. Israel invaded the Sinai Peninsula to reach the canal and found the Egyptian army ill prepared to defend against Israel's better-trained, better-supplied, and more motivated forces. In less than a week, Israel controlled the entire Sinai, but when the canal zone had been safely removed from Egyptian control, Israel was persuaded to give back most of the Sinai in exchange for a peace treaty with Egypt.

This peace lasted until 1967, when Egypt blockaded the Strait of Tiran in the Red Sea, cutting off access to the Israeli port of Elat. Nasser took this step on the basis of Soviet information (later proven false) that Israel was planning a re-invasion of the Sinai to increase its territory. At the time, Mossad, Israel's spy network, was not very good, and there was no way to determine what Nasser intended to do next. Israel made the decision to strike first—and massively—against Egypt in the event that the blockade was only the first step in an attack on Israel. This engagement became known as the Six Day War.

The Six Day War was "the most spectacular military victory in Israel's history,"[16] according to historian Avi Shlaim. In a surprise attack, Israel began the war by bombing Egyptian air bases, destroying most of its planes, and making its runways unusable. Then, unimpeded in the air, Israel's air force pummeled Egyptian land forces, making Israel's army able to advance at will. Neighboring Arab countries sided with Egypt, mostly as a means of justifying any possible opportunities to seize territory along their own borders with Israel. Israel's quick defeat of Egypt made it able to concentrate its military on its other borders, and by the end of the war, less than a week later, Israel had not only defeated Egypt and regained the Sinai and the Gaza Strip but also taken control of the Golan Heights from Syria and the West Bank from Jordan (formerly known as Transjordan).

The Emergence of the PLO

When the war was over, the United Nations passed Resolution 242, which called for a "just and lasting peace"[17] involving

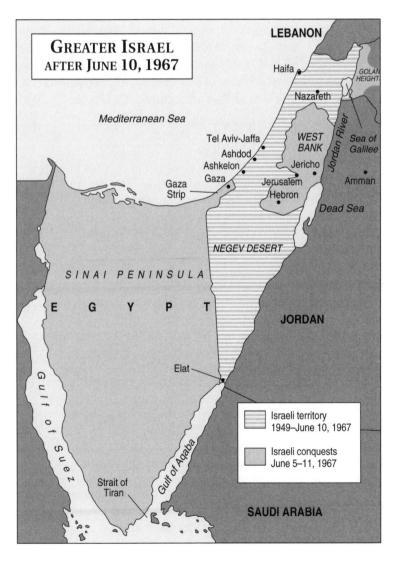

Israel's voluntary withdrawal from all its newly won land in exchange for its Arab neighbors' acceptance of its boundaries. Israel protested, citing the time-honored tradition that lands conquered in war belong to the conqueror. Its leaders saw that its boundaries would not be secure, particularly the one with Jordan, which crossed through Jerusalem itself, and felt Israel's best interest lay in keeping its new territory, primarily as a means of protecting itself. Arab countries, as a result, did not recognize Israel's legitimate existence as a nation, and thus the ongoing conflict continued. But Israel had a new image, for better or worse, in the world. No longer a beleaguered underdog in a hostile region of the world, it had become to some a bully and to others a source of admiration.

It was during this time that the United States became allied with Israel, mostly out of motivation to balance sides in the Cold War. The U.S. archenemy, the Soviet Union, had had

---

✡ DEIR YASSIN

"I have seen a great deal of war, but I never saw a sight like Deir Yassin." These words of a Haganah officer, quoted by historian Matthew Hogan in "The 1948 Massacre at Deir Yassin Revisited," refer to one of the darkest moments in Israel's history. Deir Yassin was an Arab village of stonecutters west of Jerusalem. Approximately 750 people lived in this peaceful town, getting along well with their Jewish neighbors. But Deir Yassin lay in a strategically important spot for the control of the Jerusalem–Tel Aviv corridor, so during the fighting at Kastel, when Irgun and Stern Gang irregulars approached the Haganah about helping the effort by occupying Deir Yassin, permission was rather reluctantly granted.

On April 9, 1948, a very poorly trained band of Jewish combatants, mostly teenagers, were told to take Deir Yassin. No clear instructions were given because no resistance was expected, but several Irgun and Stern Gang irregulars were killed when villagers fired on them before they gave up and fled for their lives. The young soldiers wanted to avenge their casualties, so they went into the village and started killing everyone they saw. Many of the killings were deliberately vicious and brutal; two-thirds of the victims were women, children, and the elderly. A third wave of killings took place as the soldiers began their "clean up" of the village, dispatching in cold blood anyone who had not already fled or been killed. In total, more than a hundred people were killed.

The massacre had several results, including setting off a panicked flight of Arabs into what was to be Palestinian territory, thereby initiating the refugee problem that continues today. Deir Yassin also required Israelis to look at themselves in an uncomfortable and unflattering light, and in the eyes of some, to relinquish forever the idea that there was anything holy or divinely sanctioned in the establishment of the State of Israel.

The body of an Israeli soldier killed during Israel's advance into Syria in the Six Day War.

long-standing alliances with several Middle Eastern countries, including Egypt. Fearing that other Muslim nations
could potentially be brought into the Soviet orbit, the United
States saw Israel as its only reliable ally in the region. Israel,
the Holy Land to both Jewish and Christian Americans, and
a powerful symbol to all Jews of their strength and survival
after the Holocaust, became more and more a focal point in
America's face-off against the Soviet Union during the Cold
War. Billions of dollars in foreign aid poured in to Israel to
help with its economic and military development. American

tourists came in droves. Young American Jews and others spent summers on kibbutzim, making a contribution with their hands and leaving with an even stronger emotional identification with the survival of Israel as a nation.

However, as Israel grew stronger, so did Arab hostility toward it. Egypt continued launching mortar shells across the Israeli border, and pro-Arab organizations mounted terrorist attacks designed to demoralize Israel. Among these organizations was one known as Fatah, headed by a charismatic young leader named Yasser Arafat. Another larger group, known as the Palestine Liberation Organization (PLO), soon incorporated Fatah, and Arafat became the leader of the expanded organization, which was based in Jordan. The purpose of the PLO was, from its beginning, to harass and create fear among Israelis, to demoralize them and force them to negotiate a Palestinian state. After the 1967 war, the PLO and other groups received a great deal of support from Arab countries embarrassed by their continued failure to uproot Israel by military means. Soon, however, the PLO had grown so strong that it threatened the governments of the very countries that had given it shelter. In 1970, the PLO attempted to overthrow the government of Jordan. The coup failed, and the PLO was expelled from Jordan, finding a new home in Lebanon. From its new base it escalated its program of terror, focusing on targets abroad, such as the massacre of many members of Israel's Olympic team at the games in Munich, Germany, in 1972.

PEACE WITH EGYPT

Israel's problems with Arab hostility were not limited to the actions of groups such as the PLO. In 1973, Egypt and Syria launched a two-pronged surprise attack on Israel on Yom Kippur, Judaism's most somber and important holiday. Egypt took back most of the Sinai and advanced deep into Israel. Syria threatened to conquer Israeli land as far as the Sea of Galilee, but the Israelis recouped and pushed the invaders back, recapturing the Sinai and advancing into Syria almost as far as its capital, Damascus.

This war, known most commonly as the Yom Kippur War but also known as the Ramadan War or the October War, shook Israel to the core. Although they had managed to recoup and mount a successful counteroffensive, the Israelis saw that it was really possible to be conquered. Prime Min-

Fatah leader Yasser Arafat assumed leadership of the PLO in 1968.

ister Golda Meir resigned in the wake of the Yom Kippur War because she had ignored many signals, including a direct warning from the king of Jordan to expect an imminent invasion. She had also seemed willing to let Israel absorb a deadly first strike in order to gain the sympathy of the world and, particularly, the military support of the United States.

The Egyptians and Syrians were encouraged by the outcome. "Between them," writes Avi Shlaim, "the two armies demonstrated that Israel was not invincible. They restored Arab pride, honor, and self-confidence."[18] Anwar Sadat, the Egyptian president, emerged as the strongest leader in the Arab world, the man who had taught Israel a lesson about Arab military potential. Sadat, however, understood, as did some in Israel as well, that continued warfare between his country and Israel did more harm than good. He began a personal crusade, against the strong opposition of other Arab countries and the Palestinians, to reach a lasting peace with Israel. Shlaim points out that "in all previous wars political deadlock followed the ending of hostilities. The October War was the first war to be followed by a political settlement."[19]

In 1977, Anwar Sadat personally addressed the Knesset, the Israeli parliament, and presented his plan for peace. Even though Israel thought that the plan favored Egypt too much

☆ ESCAPE AT ENTEBBE

On June 27, 1976, an Air France flight with approximately 250 people on board, flying from Tel Aviv to Paris, was hijacked by Palestinian terrorists, who boarded the plane at a layover in Athens. The plane was forced to fly to Entebbe, Uganda, then ruled by a ruthless and murderous dictator, Idi Amin, who was in on the plot. The hijackers demanded the release of Palestinian terrorists in prisons across Europe or the plane would be blown up. After a while, all passengers except Israelis and other Jews were released, but the non-Jewish captain and crew insisted on staying with the Jewish hostages.

Over the course of the next few days, the Israel Defense Forces and the government planned a daring rescue. They would send a plane carrying what they said was a negotiating team to Uganda, but behind it, flying without lights and close enough to the lead plane to confuse radar, were several other IDF planes filled with commandos and equipment, and two ready to accommodate the hostages and provide in-flight hospital care if needed. The lead plane rolled to a stop and the people on board acted as if they were on a diplomatic mission, unloading a Mercedes and escort cars that, unknown to the Ugandans, contained commandos, not negotiators. Meanwhile, in the dark behind them, the other Israeli troops were preparing a lightning assault. A fierce firefight ensued, but the attack was so well coordinated that the hostages were rescued and on board the Israeli airplane within seven minutes. Only a few IDF soldiers were killed, among them Yoni Netanyahu, brother of the future prime minister. As a sign of the small-mindedness and murderous intent of Idi Amin, the one hostage who had been wounded in the hijacking seriously enough to be hospitalized in Uganda was murdered in her bed after the rescue.

and did not accept it, Sadat's sincerity won over many Israeli citizens and leaders. A psychological barrier of mistrust seemed to have been eased. United States president Jimmy Carter took advantage of this situation to host peace talks between Sadat and Israeli prime minister Menachem Begin at the presidential retreat at Camp David in Maryland. The historic Camp David Accords were signed in 1979, providing for Israel's staged withdrawal from the rest of the Sinai in exchange for a permanent peace between the two nations. That peace, though often a tense one, has lasted to this day.

THE WAR WITH LEBANON

Historic as the Camp David Accords were, they did not bring peace to the entire region. After the PLO's relocation to Lebanon, along the Israeli border, it launched frequent artillery attacks and raids inside Israel. When the government of Lebanon did not move to effectively control the PLO, Israel invaded the PLO-dominated regions, working in alliance with a group of Lebanese called the Christian Phalangists, led by Bashir Gemayel. Gemayel and his followers were reacting to hostility prompted by both the PLO and Islamic fundamentalists in their country and wanted to overthrow the government and put Gemayel in power.

Israel at first tried to help Gemayel indirectly, so as not to appear to be meddling in the affairs of another country. But when the PLO seemed to have free rein to attack Israel without Lebanese government interference, Israel decided a direct offensive was required. The Lebanon War (1982–1985) became the most controversial in Israel's history. Though Israel claimed that the purpose of the invasion was only to push the PLO back far enough into Lebanon to put its rockets out of range of any Israeli town, Israeli forces were easily able to reach deep into Lebanon, eventually arriving in Beirut, its capital.

What Israel's real intentions were in the Lebanon War is still the subject of debate today. Israel's enemies consistently claim that its true mission was to increase its size rather than simply defend its frontiers; however, Israel had shown a willingness in the past to give back conquered land in exchange for an end to hostilities, and did so in Lebanon as well. Also disputed is the role of Ariel Sharon, who eventually became the prime minister of Israel. In one of the atrocities of that war, hundreds of Palestinians in the refugee camps at Shatilla and Sabra were slaughtered by Christian Phalangist troops. Palestinians hold Sharon responsible because, even though Israeli troops were not directly involved, the Israel Defense Forces (IDF), directed by Sharon, were aware of what was happening and clearly could have stopped the massacre but did not do so.

OPPOSITION GROWS

The Shatilla and Sabra massacres were very disheartening to Israelis. "News of the full extent of the atrocities [led] the Israeli public and the IDF to a widespread feeling of revulsion," according to historian Benny Morris. "For many Israelis, the massacre came to symbolize the war itself."[20] Although peace movements, such as Peace Now, had taken root in Israel years earlier, after these massacres they began to grow and become more vocal, holding peace rallies drawing 100,000 people or more. Whereas before, many Israelis felt the link between the will of God and the existence of the State of Israel, now many felt Israel had lost its way. What good, they asked, was the survival of a Jewish state if its citizens and leaders stopped behaving ethically as Jews? Jews believe their covenant with God gave them Israel as their Promised Land, but in return they promised to live morally, in accordance with God's commandments. The mass murder of unarmed civilians, including many children, was not at all in keeping with Judaism's understanding of God's will and, many felt, undermined the Jews' worthiness to continue to have a Jewish state.

Though Israeli politics had been characterized from the beginning by conflicting ideas about how to coexist effectively with their Arab neighbors, as the nation entered the 1990s, divisions among Israelis escalated. These divisions were over not just military policies and strategies but many other problems that had been unaddressed because the nation was forced to focus so much of its energy and resources on defense. For example, large influxes of Jewish immigrants escaping from hostile dictatorships (such as in Ethiopia and the Soviet Union) were remaining in poverty longer than previous immigrants because of an economy slowed down by military expenditures. In addition, Christian Arabs and others who had decided to remain citizens of Israel were facing ethnic discrimination. And antagonisms between ultra-Orthodox and secular Jews over a variety of issues grew more intense.

Ariel Sharon (left) with statesman Moshe Dyan, during a visit to a refugee camp in the Gaza Strip in 1971.

THE INTIFADA

While Israel dealt with its internal problems, the Palestinians had troubles of their own. The PLO had been expelled from Lebanon to the North African nation of Tunisia after bringing about the Lebanon War. Its influence appeared to be waning. Back home, Palestinian resentment was still simmering over issues such as Israel's development of its own economy without due attention to the growth of the occupied territories and the perceived exploitation of Palestinian labor by Israeli employers. Many Palestinians also resented having to subject themselves to what they considered to be harassment and humiliation at border checkpoints while commuting from the camps across the border to their jobs in Israel. The growth of Jewish communities in the West Bank and Gaza, called settlements, was also a source of anger for Palestinians; they viewed them as a sign that Israel intended to stay forever in land that the Palestinians had hoped would eventually be theirs.

In December 1987, Palestinian resentment against Israel broke loose in a spontaneous uprising that, initially, consisted mostly of screaming and shouting at Israeli troops and throwing stones and Molotov cocktails, small homemade explosives. This popular movement became known as the Intifada (which in Arabic means a throwing or a shaking off of something unwanted). Strikes, boycotts, and sporadic violence against Israelis continued for several years. Ambitious politicians, including Yasser Arafat, operating from Tunis, jockeyed for recognition as the head of an essentially leaderless movement of people on the street.

Arafat's dilemma was that he knew that to be recognized by the world as the leader of the Palestinian people, he would have to be willing to negotiate a solution to the Palestinian and Israeli standoff. However, he also knew that many fundamentalist Muslims, including the group known as Hamas, would never accept a leader who was willing to compromise. Though the bombings and other forms of terrorism against Israeli citizens were beyond the control of any one person, a concerned world looked to a Palestinian leader to offer a chance for a solution. Arafat was able to reassure the world that peace was possible and that he personally would work for it, while at the same time not alarming or antagonizing the increasingly restless and angry Palestinians who seemed

Israeli soldiers restrain a Palestinian youth suspected of throwing stones.

to be willing to settle for nothing less than the destruction of Israel. Arafat gradually became the recognized leader of the Palestinians in the eyes of the world and the Palestinians themselves, and his PLO was viewed as the organization by which Palestinians would end their perceived oppression.

The stage was now set for a new decade, the 1990s, a time when the inconsistencies of talking about peace but tolerating violence would often characterize the leadership of both sides. Israel had been formed only four decades before by a people united, despite their differences, by a singular vision of making their homeland bloom and prosper. Indeed, in many respects, it had. But as the 1990s dawned, the peace and human harmony at the core of the Jewish vision of the Promised Land were threatened by dissension from inside the Jewish community and growing hostility from outside, and peace seemed as unachievable as ever.

Building Up and Breaking Down: The Struggle for Peace and Prosperity

The decade of the 1990s got off to a turbulent start all around the globe with the sudden collapse of the Soviet Union and the end of the Cold War. During the four decades of the Cold War, poorer and less powerful nations around the world had been able to increase their regional influence and develop their economies by allying themselves with either the United States or the Soviet Union in exchange for monetary aid. Without Soviet military might behind them, Middle Eastern nations allied with that side no longer had the means to threaten Israel, and thus the 1990s seemed to offer the prospect of a lasting peace in the region. In fact, through the first half of the 1990s, peace seemed close at hand on a number of occasions, only to slip away as a result of fear, mistrust, and deep-seated anger on both sides. Though economically the decade was a good one for Israel, it ended with a destructive new Palestinian Intifada, and peace very far away indeed.

A Chance for Peace at Madrid

In late 1991, Israel and Syria joined representatives of the Palestinians in Spain at the Madrid Peace Conference to discuss resolving the Palestinian problem. However, Israelis had learned to be wary of dealing with Yasser Arafat, because of his record of talking about peace while using the resources of the PLO to fund and otherwise encourage acts of terrorism against Israel. As a result, even while the peace talks were going on, Israel continued actively encouraging Israelis to live in the West Bank and the Golan Heights and to develop business, industry, and agriculture there, establishing what defense minister and famed army general Moshe Dayan once described as "facts on the ground"[21] about their intention to stay. Many Israelis favored this approach, but to the Palestinians, the settlements were simply proof of Israel's lack of concern for them as a homeless people. Land in the West Bank and Gaza could be, and many argued should be, part of a Palestinian state. The more Israel developed the area, the slimmer the chances were that it would ever give it up. In the end, the Madrid talks ended unsuccessfully largely because of this issue.

THE OSLO ACCORDS

Despite what for many was the disappointment of Madrid, the next few years were good ones on the political front for Israel. A new prime minister, Yitzhak Rabin, who had made his mark on Israeli history as a young officer during the War of Independence, was elected in 1992. Although he had been in the military, by the time of his election, Rabin had begun to lose faith in armed force as the best way to keep Israel safe. Soon after his election, and unknown to the Israeli public, Rabin started secret negotiations with the PLO in Oslo, Norway. Secrecy was needed because whenever there were signs that a negotiated peace process might be reached, terrorist groups such as Hamas would derail the process by stepping up violence, and Knesset members opposing compromise would introduce bills or call for votes designed to tie the hands of the Israeli negotiators.

Israeli negotiators (left) meet with the Palestinian–Jordanian delegation in Madrid, Spain, in 1991.

✡ THE ETHIOPIAN AIRLIFTS

Jews in Israel and around the world are proud of their record in keeping to the vision of Israel as a homeland for all the world's Jews. Some immigrants have simply arrived on their own, but others have been brought through campaigns financed in significant part by American Jewish groups and carried out by the Israeli government. Jews first demonstrated this commitment in the first three years of the nation's existence, when 50,000 Yemenite and 120,000 Iraqi Jews were airlifted out of hostile countries in Operation Magic Carpet and Operation Ezra. In 1989, Operation Exodus brought 700,000 Soviet Jews to Israel.

Perhaps the most famous of these campaigns was a series of airlifts that rescued Ethiopia's Jews from starvation during a long period of drought. The first airlift, Operation Moses, evacuated fifteen thousand Ethiopian Jews in less than thirty-six hours from refugee camps in the Sudan in 1984. The second, Operation Solomon, in 1991, had to be planned and carried out as a top-secret mission because of the hostile Ethiopian government. The Israeli airline El Al and the Israeli air force used many planes to swoop in and, within hours, evacuate twenty thousand Ethiopian Jews.

Ethiopian immigrants have had some unique problems in Israel. First, many were not recognized as Jews because they went to Africa very early in Jewish history and developed in isolation from mainstream Jewry. Although they followed the Torah, they did not know about centuries of rabbinic rulings and teachings that had shaped the faith for other Jews. A scandal erupted over secret ceremonies conducted by rabbis to "convert" the new arrivals as they stepped off the planes, but even though that practice stopped, their assimilation into Israel was not a smooth one. First, they barely eked out a living as farmers and herders in Ethiopia, and they completely lacked job skills for Israel. Many were illiterate. This made them very different from most other Jews coming to Israel. Even today, nearly twenty years later, many still live in poverty, with unemployment rates three times the national average. An estimated three-quarters of Ethiopian Jews cannot write Hebrew, and as many as half do not speak it well. For many Ethiopians, however, the army has served as a way of improving their lives, and more than fifty Ethiopians now serve as officers in the IDF.

In 1993, the Oslo Accords were announced. The accords were a declaration of principles that would serve as the foundation for negotiating and planning a permanent peace. The Oslo Accords set a timeline for a phased withdrawal of Israeli troops from territories held since the 1967 war and established the Palestinian National Authority (PNA) as the governing body in the West Bank and Gaza Strip. Thorny issues such as the future of the settlements and who would end up in control of Jerusalem were to be negotiated over the next few years, with all issues to be decided by the target date of 1998. It was a major step forward that allowed for the possibility of peaceful conditions to prevail before every last detail was worked out.

A HERO FALLS

The Oslo Accords introduced at least cautious optimism into Israeli life. Rabin was perceived by many as the right leader at the right time to fashion what might be a lasting peace. Within an atmosphere of deep mutual mistrust, Rabin and Arafat continued to make progress toward peace. Israel withdrew from the Gaza Strip and portions of the West Bank, and the PNA, led by Arafat, became the official governing body in those areas. Tragically, once again, the hopes of the Israelis, and many Palestinians as well, were dashed when Rabin was assassinated in 1995, not by an Arab but by an Israeli, Yigal Amir. Amir claimed that he had "acted to save the Jewish people"[22] by stopping a peace process that would have involved giving up land he considered promised to the Jews by God.

Israeli security personnel push Yitzhak Rabin into a car after a right-wing Jewish law student shot him in 1995. Rabin later died of his injuries.

The country was devastated, brought to a complete halt by its grief. Several million Israelis participated in rallies to honor their fallen leader. Many were not ready to call his death the end to the process he had started, however, so under the next prime minister, Shimon Peres, negotiations continued and Israeli troops continued to withdraw from parts of the West Bank, including the cities of Bethlehem, Jenin, and Ramallah. The PNA held elections and removed from official documents all references to the goal of the destruction of Israel.

A NEW TURN TO THE RIGHT

There was by no means unanimous support for these peace efforts on either side. Some Palestinians had boycotted the PNA elections in protest of any compromises with Israel, and Rabin's assassination by an Israeli showed clearly that not all Israelis favored making peace with the Palestinians. Surprisingly, one year after the huge rallies in the wake of Rabin's death, Benjamin Netanyahu, a right-wing politician from the Likud Party, was elected prime minister based on his opposition to any concession of land for peace. His election was a sign that the negotiations with the Palestinians had gone too far too fast for the Israeli public.

Netanyahu claimed to be willing to go along with all previous deals reached by Rabin and Peres with Arafat, but, in fact, he slowed down the peace negotiations as much as he could. He argued publicly that "statements made in the course of negotiations which are not written down . . . are *not* formal commitments. . . . I will only honor formal commitments."[23] According to historians Ahron Bregman and Jihan El-Tahri, "For Netanyahu, when Peres . . . promised little he had promised too much." Netanyahu "took steps that killed the spirit of Oslo and infuriated the Palestinians."[24] His support for expansion of settlements increased tensions. It seemed as if Netanyahu was determined to feign interest in negotiations while pursuing a path that made their success impossible, just as the Israelis had accused Arafat of doing.

During Netanyahu's time as prime minister, he was embroiled in several scandals, and his arrogant and abrasive personality earned him little loyalty. In 1999, after three years in power, he was forced to call an early election, which he lost to Ehud Barak, the Labor Party candidate. Barak lasted only nineteen months, after which Ariel Sharon, an old soldier whose lasting animosity toward Arafat could be traced back to the war in Lebanon, won the prime minister's job with a convincing 60 percent of the popular vote.

NEW INTIFADA, AN OLD RESPONSE

As a result of the constant bickering between interest groups, Sharon's government, like those before, has been unable to implement coherent and consistent policies on the economy, the settlements, and other issues. However, Sharon has remained quite popular as a result of his "get tough" strategies during a new Intifada declared in 2000. This Intifada, which continued unabated in 2002, was different from the last one in that its focus was not strikes or street demonstrations but suicide bombings aimed at killing Israeli citizens.

"A STAND AGAINST VIOLENCE AND FOR PEACE": YITZHAK RABIN

Yitzhak Rabin, the first native-born prime minister of Israel, had fought in the Palmach, the elite strike force of the Haganah during the War of Independence, and later had become an IDF general. His work on the Oslo Accords had put his nation on the path to peace, but he himself fell victim to violence. For many Israelis, Rabin is the greatest of national heroes, and his death one of the major turning points in Israeli history.

To the cheers of hundreds of thousands gathered in Tel Aviv on November 4, 1995, for a national rally honoring him, Prime Minister Yitzhak Rabin said to the crowd (excerpted here from the website of the Israeli Ministry of Foreign Affairs),

> Permit me to say I am deeply moved. I wish to thank each and every one of you who has come here today to take a stand against violence and for peace . . . a peace that will solve most of Israel's problems. I was a military man for 27 years. I fought so long as there was no chance for peace. I believe there is now a chance for peace—a great chance. We must take advantage of it for the sake of those standing here and for those who are not here. Violence erodes the basis of Israeli democracy. It must be condemned and isolated. This is not the way of the State of Israel. Peace opens the door to a better economy and society. Peace is not just a prayer. It is also the aspiration of the Jewish people. There are enemies of peace who are trying to hurt us to torpedo the peace process. This is a course that is fraught with difficulties and with pain. In Israel there is no path that is without pain. But the path of peace is preferable to the path of war. I say this to you as a former military man who sees the pain of the families of the IDF soldiers. For them, for our children, in my case for my grandchildren, I want this government to exhaust every opening, every possibility to promote and achieve a comprehensive peace. This rally must send a message to the Israeli people, to the Jewish people around the world, to the many people in the Arab world, and indeed to the entire world, that the Israeli people want peace, support peace. For this I thank you.

Rabin left the stage after saying these words. They would be his last. As the prime minister entered his car, an assassin shot him dead, and a shocked nation had to come to grips with the fact that a Jew could be one of the "enemies of peace" of which Rabin had just spoken.

One of these bombings, on the Jewish holiday of Passover in 2002, killed twenty-nine people in Netanya as they were sitting down to begin their celebration of one of the most significant holidays of the Jewish year.

Within a few days of that event, the Israeli army reoccupied most of the West Bank, laying siege to Arafat's headquarters in Ramallah. Arafat became an overnight hero to those who saw Israel as the oppressor of Palestinians. Ironically, these events enhanced his stature, which had diminished considerably in recent years among his own people and around the world. Arafat was accused of many human rights violations against his opponents and even of directly sponsoring and funding terrorist acts in Israel. He was also embroiled in scandals involving giving foreign aid intended for impoverished Palestinians living in refugee camps to members of his inner circle. But all such problems were put aside in the eyes of many Palestinians and sympathizers around the world, replaced by television images of Arafat being interviewed by flashlight inside his besieged compound. In the end, the siege was lifted without any real apparent gain for Israel or the Palestinian people.

Two other important events took center stage during the 2002 military occupation of the West Bank. The Jenin refugee camp, where a number of wanted Palestinian terrorists lived, was surrounded, and a house-to-house search resulted in fatalities on both sides. When a section of the camp was bulldozed, the international press covered the story intensively, including the insistence by the Palestinians that a massacre had occurred that Israel was trying to hide. Investigators concluded that there had been no massacre and that fewer than a

Israeli soldiers block the entrance to Arafat's Ramallah headquarters in July 2002.

hundred Palestinians had died, mostly in combat. Israelis pointed to the fact that they had not shelled or bombed Jenin specifically to keep Palestinian casualties low and that the more dangerous door-to-door search had cost a number of young Israeli soldiers their lives. However, Jenin became yet another public relations nightmare for Israel despite these precautions.

The other important incident was a siege at the Church of the Nativity in Bethlehem, reputedly built over the site where Jesus Christ was born. Wanted Palestinians barricaded themselves inside the church for more than a month. Press coverage focused on the plight of those inside, which included priests and a few others who just happened to have been there when the siege began. Though some pointed out that the sacredness of the place was violated by the armed men holed up inside more than by the Israeli tanks in the square, international opinion favored the Palestinians.

THE IMPASSE CONTINUES

It was hard to see either side as a winner in the escalation of tensions between Israel and the Palestinians in 2002. Israel showed that it could move at will in the West Bank to round up suspected terrorists and that it was willing to go against world opinion and its allies to protect its interests. Arafat was allowed to stay in the territories, though there was talk of expelling him, on the condition that he reorganize his government to minimize corruption and human rights abuse and that he rein in terrorists going into Israel to harm civilians. Israel in return withdrew its troops from around the cities of the West Bank.

However, the suicide bombings did not stop, and for every successfully carried out bombing, many more were foiled by Israeli intelligence. Few believed that Arafat had the power, even if he had the will, to stop the bombings. Arafat was forced to make reforms within his organization to prove to the world that he was capable of being a leader of an independent nation. Yet Israelis feel they have seen it all before and that Arafat must somehow be removed from power and possibly expelled from Israeli territory as a precondition for any meaningful peace talks. To this point, that has not happened, in large part because Israel wants to maintain the support of the United States and other allies that are reluctant to endorse the overthrow of an elected leader, regardless of the situation.

As their lives continue to be disrupted by random violence, Israelis yearn for peace. They are tired of wondering whether they or someone they love will be the next to die in a suicide bombing. They know that military force only achieves short lulls in the violence and is not a solution. Israelis look for options and do not see many. Most simply try to go on with their daily lives without any real hope of change. A good day is one without violence. A stable future seems as elusive as ever.

An Israeli soldier secures a rooftop near Bethlehem's Church of the Nativity (right) in May 2002.

5

DAILY LIFE IN ISRAEL

Daily life in Israel, as anywhere else in the world, centers around a few important places—work, school, and home. In Israel, several other key elements, most notably the military and religious institutions, also play a large role in daily life. Though these five aspects of life are the foundation of a national experience and identity, how people go about prioritizing these elements is an indication of how diverse Israelis really are.

A JEWISH STATE

Any discussion of Israeli identity must begin with the fact that Israel is a Jewish state—the only land in the world where Jews are, or ever have been, the majority. Although Israel is a democracy, it is also a theocracy, a nation where religious rules are at the heart of government. The prime minister, Knesset (the Israeli parliament), and judges have the latitude to make policy, pass legislation, and issue verdicts, as long as their decisions do not violate any religious law laid down in the Torah.

As a result, one might think that Israelis as a whole regularly go to synagogues and observe religious rituals and rules, but this is not the case. Considering the nation's history and its unique status as a Jewish state, it comes as a surprise to many people to learn that only approximately 20 percent of Israeli Jews are highly observant, as measured by such things as weekly attendance at synagogues, following kosher dietary laws, and regular prayer. Most of the rest are proud to call themselves Jews by culture and heritage but do not see religious observance as important in their lives.

THE JEWISH YEAR

Regardless of whether they call themselves "religious," the Jews of Israel organize their year around the Jewish holidays.

The Jewish year begins in the fall with Rosh Hashanah, the beginning of an eight-day period known as the High Holidays that ends with Yom Kippur, the Day of Atonement. The High Holidays are an opportunity for self-reflection about the year, a chance to ask forgiveness for wrongdoing and atone for mistakes. After Yom Kippur is the harvest festival of Succot, followed by Hanukkah, considered a minor holiday, occurring in December. Another minor spring holiday, Purim, celebrated similarly to Halloween in the United States, is in early spring.

The second most important Jewish holiday after the High Holidays is Pesach (Passover), the spring holiday commemorating the release of the Hebrews from slavery in Egypt. After Pesach, a period of seven weeks passes before the last major holiday of the Jewish year, Shavuot, a spring harvest festival. All these holidays involve days off from work, their greatest significance for many Israelis. Important Christian events, however, are not observed as national holidays. Christmas, for example, is a regular workday, just as Rosh Hashanah is a regular workday in other countries.

A Jewish boy reads from a prayer book during a traditional bar mitzvah ceremony.

Several other important holidays have more recent roots, including Independence Day and Yom HaShoah, a commemoration of the 6 million Jews murdered in the Holocaust. At a particular time on that day, air raid sirens sound and everyone in Israel stops what they are doing. Even cars

---

✡ KEEPING KOSHER

Adhering to dietary laws laid down in the Torah is an essential part of the practice of Judaism. The laws of kashruth (kosher) food preparation and consumption are very complex, but have several essential components. First, certain foods cannot be eaten at all. This includes pork, shellfish, game animals, and any fish (such as eel or shark) that does not have both fins and scales. Second, dairy and meat products cannot be eaten together. Roast beef, for example, could not be served with mashed potatoes made with milk, nor could turkey be combined with cheese in a sandwich. Likewise, at a barbecue where chicken was on the menu, corn on the cob would have to be served without butter. Dairy and meat cannot be served even in separate dishes during the same meal. Kosher-observant Jews generally try to keep the two foods from ever being in the stomach at the same time; for example, after eating a piece of chicken, they would wait to have a scoop of ice cream for as long as six hours.

For a cow or chicken to be kosher, it must be slaughtered in a particular way. A specially trained butcher using special instruments, including an extremely sharp knife free from nicks of any sort, kills the animal and ensures that all the blood is drained from it, in keeping with the biblical idea that the blood contains the life spirit and thus would be unholy to eat. "Kashering," which includes salting and brining, draws off additional blood. The animal must be determined to have been free from disease or defect as well, and only permissible parts of the animal may be used.

Laws against eating certain combinations of food also apply to food preparation, utensils, and dishes. A kosher kitchen contains different sets of pots and pans, knives, bowls, silverware, dishes, and even tablecloths for dairy and for meat so that no residues will ever be inadvertently mixed.

Kosher-observant Jews believe that the table at which a family eats is a kind of altar and that being careful about what and how they eat is an acknowledgment of God and his blessings.

A traditional Passover Seder meal, commemorating the Jewish exodus from Egypt.

on the freeway stop, and their occupants get out to stand with bowed heads in memory of lost lives.

SHABBAT

Even more than the holidays, the central event of the Jewish calendar is Shabbat, the Sabbath, which lasts from sundown Friday to sundown Saturday. At sundown, it is a woman's duty to light special candles and recite a blessing, which signals the official beginning of Shabbat. The evening is spent having a special meal, during which many more blessings are recited. For observant Jews, all work is forbidden on the Sabbath. (Work is generally defined as anything that creates something of lasting value, such as writing a letter or making a purchase, or something that interferes in any way with the natural order of things, such as lighting a fire, pruning a rosebush, or even driving a car.) Special traditional foods (and ways to keep them warm) have evolved from the necessity of preparing all Sabbath food before sundown on Friday. In Jerusalem and in many other cities and towns, public transportation is shut down for Shabbat, and many stores and restaurants are closed as well. Restaurants that remain open forfeit their right to have a kosher certificate, which means that no observant Jew will eat there even during the week. Israelis, whether they observe Shabbat or not, are used to the routine and the restrictions. As a result, to get necessary tasks done before sundown, the pace of business is particularly brisk on Friday afternoons.

The Saturday of Shabbat is spent studying, participating in family events such as going to a park, attending services at the synagogue, and, for adults, the traditional, much-cherished afternoon nap. Even though Shabbat is a special and valued time, most people look forward to nightfall on Saturday night, when, after another set of blessings is recited, Shabbat is over for another week. Saturday evening is a popular time for going to the movies, restaurants, and nightclubs or just for taking a walk along crowded pedestrian streets or having a coffee in the town square. For Israelis, their Saturday night activities mark the end of the weekend. Israelis typically work and go to school from Sunday to the early afternoon on Friday.

Christians gather outside Jerusalem in celebration of Palm Sunday, a celebration held the Sunday before Easter.

NON-JEWISH ISRAEL

Arab Israelis converse near a market in Haifa.

Though the patterns of the Israel week are decidedly Jewish, many other groups have their own traditions. The non-Jewish population of Israel is made up of a number of very different groups. Most are Arabs, divided into Christians and Muslims, with a small subset of Druze. Druze practice their own mysterious and secretive faith—so secret that many Druze themselves do not know all of its rules and beliefs. The Arabs are just as likely as the Jews to be nonpracticing. However, despite the fact that the typical resident of Israel is not terribly focused on his or her faith, Jews, Muslims, Christians, and others nevertheless have very distinct practices that make them very different from each other in their customs and daily life.

Christians adhere to the Christian calendar of holidays, including a Sunday Sabbath, putting religiously observant Christians at odds with the rhythms of Israeli life. The majority of the Christians in Israel are ethnic Arabs, although small numbers of European and other Christians, often doing church-related work, live in the Holy Land as well.

Official Israeli policy is to tolerate all religions, so Muslims are also free to worship and live as they wish. Haifa, for example, has a large Muslim population and a beautiful mosque that serves as a center for worship. In Arab villages, which dot the landscape all over Israel, the sounds of the

Muslim call to prayer fill the air five times a day. As with Christians, it is common for Muslims to educate their children outside the Israeli public school system for religious reasons, and the different holidays and observances tend to keep observant Israeli Muslims out of the mainstream of Israeli life.

ISRAELI COMMUNITIES

Religion is not the only source of diversity, however. Though many Israelis live in apartment complexes in cities and suburbs, or in small towns and villages all over the country, Jewish Israelis also live in several unique kinds of communities not usually found elsewhere. The kibbutz is an Israeli invention. Kibbutzim were founded by early Zionist socialists, who believed that the way to build a Jewish homeland was through communities that would labor together to make the land yield crops. The kibbutz owned all food, clothing, housing, and other necessities, and people simply took what they required from a central supply source. Cash was rarely needed for anything, but if it was, kibbutz members could simply take the money from a small community-owned account.

Many Jews from around the world emigrated in the first decade or two after the establishment of the nation specifically to be part of the kibbutz lifestyle. Today's kibbutzim are still run in much the same manner, but the days of hopping onto tractors together at dawn to go out to tend the fields are largely gone, and there is a little more room for private ownership of goods. Most kibbutzim also make ends meet by other means today, such as operating tourist holiday camps and hotels or opening an industrial operation of some sort.

Another kind of Israeli community is the settlement. Typically, these are suburbs of large cities or small towns in disputed territories such as the Golan Heights and the West Bank. The settlements are politically controversial, and some people go to live in them to make a statement that these lands are a legitimate part of Israel. Others live in settlements not for political reasons but because they cannot afford housing elsewhere. They form a sizable commuter population, dashing between gates of their fenced and guarded community along the often-dangerous roads to their work in Jerusalem or elsewhere.

Many other Israelis live in small villages, usually of one ethnic group or another. Israeli Arab villages are scattered all over Israel. Many of these villages thrive on Jewish customers who come to eat in the restaurants or shop in the stores on the Sabbath, or to buy items such as pork and shellfish, which cannot be sold in kosher grocery stores. Even in the midst of suicide bombings elsewhere, the relationship between Jews and Arabs seems untroubled in these villages, proof that human relationships are always more complex than news headlines would lead outsiders to think.

SCHOOL

Regardless of what kind of community they live in, with few exceptions, children attend school from the age of five for

---

✡ THE *ULPAN*

Hebrew is a difficult language for immigrants to learn. It has its own alphabet that is used in no other language except Yiddish, a language used by Jews in eastern Europe. Hebrew is written from right to left, and books are read from back to front. Grammatically, it has many unusual features, such as the absence of the present tense verb "to be" in sentences such as *Ata talmid* ("He student"). The attachment of letters to the beginnings and ends of words is handled very differently than in English. For example, "my aunt" is structured as one word, *dodati* ("auntmy"); David and Sarah would be written as *David veSarah* ("David andSarah"); and "the book" is written as *hasefer* ("thebook").

To help new immigrants and others interested in learning Hebrew, schools of language instruction known as *ulpanim* have evolved. In an *ulpan* (the singular form), students receive crash courses of varying intensity and focus. Some are short courses concentrating only on the Hebrew necessary to conduct daily life. Others last as long as four or five hours six days a week to provide students with a thorough knowledge of Hebrew reading, writing, and speaking. Professionals from Russia and other countries often take these courses to help them in their professions in their new home. Many *ulpanim* are state run and offer free instruction to new *aliyot*, as immigrants are known. Private *ulpanim* abound as well, and institutions such as Hebrew University in Jerusalem often offer their own crash courses to enable new students to learn effectively in Hebrew.

An Orthodox Jewish boy studies in a private school in Jerusalem.

twelve years. School runs Sunday through Friday except in summer, and children study subjects similar to those in the United States. Most Israeli schoolchildren study English as well. Because only 2 percent of the world's population is Jewish, and many of those do not speak Hebrew, learning another language is considered essential to students' overall ability to communicate. Students are free to choose other languages, but English is by far the most commonly studied, and most Israelis have at least some degree of familiarity with it.

The children of the extremely Orthodox Haredi Jews do not go to public schools. Instead, they study at the yeshiva in their neighborhood or at home. The focus of their education is the Torah, and most other learning is considered to be a distraction and a waste of time. They learn to read and write biblical Hebrew, but they do not speak it. They speak primarily Yiddish, the language of the Jews of eastern Europe, which is a mix of Hebrew, German, Polish, and Russian. Haredi and other Jews who are lumped together as Hasidic have very little contact with people outside their community; Hasidic women are raised mostly at home to take on their eventual duties as wives and mothers.

MILITARY SERVICE

Military service in Israel is compulsory for nearly everyone. The ultra-Orthodox population is one of the few groups excused from military service, in part because the religious requirements of their lifestyle would make serving difficult. Arabs may also ask to be excused from the army rather than fight against their own people, although many do join the vast majority of Israelis who complete military service. Even new immigrants who do not speak Hebrew must serve; they generally spend the first part of their period of service, however, in special schools known as *ulpanim* to learn the language. Israelis take military service in stride. Recently, though, a movement has developed to refuse to serve in the West Bank, Golan Heights, or Gaza Strip, because many perceive Israeli communities there as illegal or at least contrary to any hope of peace with the Palestinians.

Young men are required to serve in the military for three years following high school graduation, and young women for two. Service is to be completed by their twenty-first birthday, so most immediately join, but others take a year off after high school. Only males are assigned to combat duty. It is traditional for military service to include activities designed to promote appreciation for the nation of Israel, so young people who do not directly remember the lives that were lost fighting for independence or the millions lost in the Holocaust will develop a clear sense of how important it is to fight to the death if necessary to preserve the nation. All soldiers, for example, spend a day at Yad Vashem, the Holocaust Memorial and Museum, and many have ceremonies marking the completion of basic training at inspiring sites such as Masada and the Western Wall. In this way, the oft-repeated phrase, in reference to the Holocaust, "never again" is carried on to future generations.

For the most part, new soldiers serve willingly and proudly. The purpose of the active-duty members of the Israel Defense Forces, as the armed services are known, is to hold the front lines until the reserves, far greater in numbers, can be mobilized to carry on the fight. After active duty, Israeli males serve in the reserves for years, until their late fifties. If their units are called up, they are expected to drop what they are doing and report within hours. This they generally do with good spirits, and they sometimes arrive so quickly that preparations for them are incomplete, and they remain cold and hungry until the IDF can take care of their basic needs.

Those called for reserve duty are generally people whose regular army service was in combat units. They can be called as often as once a year for a month. Laws have evolved to protect the jobs of those called to duty, but there is no doubt that the economy and activities of the country suffer tremendously when the reserves are mobilized. Lawyers leave cases unfinished, businessmen leave contracts un-concluded, engineers and architects call a halt to projects,

✡ YAD VASHEM

Yad Vashem, visited by all Israeli soldiers as part of their training, is a hilltop memorial to the more than 6 million Jews killed during World War II. It consists of gardens, monuments, and a museum devoted to various aspects of the Holocaust. One of these, the Children's Memorial, is dedicated to the 1.5 million Jewish children who were killed by the Nazis. Visitors pass enlarged photographs of a handful of victims and enter a dark room lit only by a few candles. These candles are reflected in a series of mirrors that leave the impression of a galaxy of golden starlight. Walking through the room, the visitor is left with a sense of the unfathomable loss of these children's spirits and potential contributions to the world.

Another memorial is the Hall of Remembrance, a stark room made of blocks of basalt, a dark but luminous stone. In the center is an eternal flame, surrounded by the carved names of the twenty-one death camps, including Auschwitz and Bergen-Belsen, where Anne Frank, author of the famous diary, died of typhus shortly before the camp was liberated. Also at Yad Vashem are memorial gardens, including the Avenue of the Righteous Gentiles and the Valley of the Lost Communities, featuring dramatic and powerful statues, trees, and flowers. Indoors, visitors can view art exhibits of items such as toys found at the death camps and art created by concentration camp prisoners.

An Israeli soldier guards the Jaffa gate, one of the entrances to the ancient walled city of Jerusalem.

and countless others simply cease their contributions to the work the country requires to keep it going.

Because mobilization is frequent, rapid, and temporary, the military in Israel has a rather informal style. Soldiers use cell phones to call girlfriends, wives, and parents from their stations, and many try to conduct business while waiting for something interesting to happen. Soldiers with long hair are a common sight. Parents and friends show up to bring better food and just a few minutes of familiar company, and spirits tend to be high despite the grumbling. There is indeed a sense that everyone in Israel must play a role in the nation's survival.

6

COMMON ROOTS AND CREATIVE VISIONS: ARTS AND CULTURE IN ISRAEL

Perhaps no single work of art in Israel better symbolizes the themes that characterize the arts and culture in Israel today than the twelve stained glass windows in the synagogue of Hadassah Hospital at Ein Kerem, near Jerusalem. They were completed in 1982 by one of the twentieth century's most important artists, Marc Chagall, a Russian Jew. Chagall chose as his theme the twelve sons of the patriarch Jacob, designing each window with bold, bright swirls and splashes of color and a few identifiable symbols such as the lion, representing Jacob's son Judah. The overall effect is a dazzling dance of colors and shapes, an entirely original take on an ancient subject. Though he did not live in Israel, Chagall felt a deep connection with his ancient roots there: "All the time I was working, I felt my father and my mother were looking over my shoulder, and behind them were Jews, millions of other vanished Jews of yesterday and a thousand years ago."[25] The Chagall Windows are prime examples of how the ancient children of Israel continue to inspire their descendants today to create vibrant new art reflective of their identity as Jews.

VISUAL AND DECORATIVE ARTS

Jewish culture has always been characterized by a love of the arts. Talents such as playing musical instruments were encouraged even among the poor. The early Zionists knew that life would be hard in Palestine, but they also knew that any Jewish homeland would have to have artists, musicians, and poets. In keeping with this idea, the Zionist Assembly decided in 1905 to set up an art academy in Jerusalem under the direction of renowned artist Boris Shatz. The Bezalel Academy of Arts and Crafts opened its doors in 1906; its purpose was to encourage young artists to immigrate and develop distinctive art that could be marketed around the world. Within less than five years, the Bezalel Academy had five hundred students in thirty-two departments, and it remained the greatest single influence on the development of Israeli art for several decades.

Bezalel-trained artists in Israel took as their main subject matter the stark beauty and subtle colors of the desert landscapes. But during World War II and after, the traumas of the Holocaust and the continued strains of life in a war-torn country caused some Israeli artists to choose different themes, such as suffering and injustice. Others, such as Marcel Janco and Avigdo Arikha, reached back to their ancient roots to develop themes and symbols from biblical times. In more recent years, Israeli artists have been innovative in

The stained glass artistry of Russian Jewish artist Marc Chagall.

their use of mixed media, such as collages, and have experimented with the creative use of Jewish symbols such as candles, the Star of David, and letters of the Hebrew alphabet in their work. Some of the best-known contemporary Israeli artists are Pinchas Cohen-Gan, Deganit Beresht, Gabi Klazmer, and Tsvi Goldstein.

Israel also has an outstanding array of talented artisans. Many Israeli ceramists, potters, silver- and goldsmiths, jewelry makers, glassblowers, and weavers have international reputations. They often focus on integrating Jewish themes and symbols into their works or creating beautiful and inno-

This woodcut by Jewish artist Jacob Steinhardt depicts the biblical story of Noah and the Flood.

EIN HOD

Near Haifa, at the base of Mount Carmel, overlooking the Mediterranean, lies the artists' colony of Ein Hod. Shortly after the War of Independence, a small group of artists led by Marcel Janco, a painter, decided that the little abandoned town with its crusader ruins and beautiful views would make a perfect place to live communally and build their studios. Over the years, the colony grew, and now there are approximately one hundred artists who live in and around the area. The artists of Ein Hod still live communally, making decisions in a general council and an administrative committee. The visual artists all exhibit work at the main gallery, the largest in Israel. Other artists such as musicians and dancers put on a number of performances that draw in Israeli visitors and tourists from around the world.

vative objects such as candlesticks, prayer shawls, and dishes used for holidays and religious rituals. As a result, the work of Israeli artisans is much in demand by Jews around the world, as well as by discerning tourists, making Israeli crafts a significant part of the country's economy.

LITERATURE AND FILM

The roots of tradition run very deep in all the arts in Israel. Jews remain linked to their past as a result of their ancestors' desire to preserve in writing the details of their people and their faith. The Hebrew Bible, known to Christians as the Old Testament and to Jews as the *Tanakh,* is also appreciated by Jews and non-Jews alike for its poetry, and it has served as the foundation for the revival of literature written in Hebrew in modern times. Since early Zionist Eliezer Ben-Yehuda demonstrated that Hebrew could be the language of Jewish Palestine, Hebrew grew rapidly in its written forms, beginning with daily newspapers and rising to produce 1966 Nobel Prize–winning author Shmuel Yosef Agnon (1888–1970). Agnon, an Orthodox Jew who learned Hebrew as a second language when he immigrated, was the most prominent member of the first generation of writers in modern Hebrew. His works explored themes such as loss of religious faith and the struggle to live ethically in troubled times; he wrote

Famed Hebrew writer Shmuel Yosef Agnon in 1966.

groundbreaking works such as *The Bridal Canopy* and *A Guest for the Night* as well as numerous short stories and novellas.

Unlike Agnon, the next generation of writers were native Hebrew speakers, most born in Palestine at the time of the British mandate. These novelists wrote in a variety of styles on many themes, often addressing social problems at home and abroad as tensions mounted both locally with the Arabs and in Europe with the rise of Hitler. The next generation, coming of age in the 1960s and 1970s, includes several of the best-known Israeli fiction writers, including internationally acclaimed Amos Oz. Oz has been a prolific writer of fiction and nonfiction dealing with the lives of ordinary individuals struggling with the challenges of life in Israel. An active member of Peace Now, Oz is a major spokesperson for pacifism in Israel today.

Other well-known writers in the last several decades include A.B. Yehoshua, Aharon Appelfeld, David Shahar, Meir Shalev, and David Grossman. Women such as Amalia Kahana-Carmon, Hannah Bat-Shaharm, and Ruth Almog have also made a significant mark. Voices of smaller communities within Israel have been represented as well. Anton Shammas provides the viewpoint of a Christian Arab, and Yossl Birstein writes about life in the ultra-Orthodox Jewish communities of Israel.

Poets are also well represented among writers in modern Hebrew. Rachel Bluwstein, known simply as Rachel, was the first major Jewish poet of the Zionist era, writing short, emotional poems that had a great influence on later women poets such as Dalia Ravikovitch and Maya Bejerano. Yehuda

Amichai, whose death in 2000 was widely mourned in Israel, and Dan Pagis are two of the best-known poets of recent years. Meir Wieseltier, Yair Hurvitz, and Yona Wallach have established themselves as significant figures for the next generation. Israeli poets today, like their counterparts all over the world, write in a wide variety of styles, ranging from tightly structured verse to wildly innovative expression. Their subject matter varies from serious political and social issues, to matters of the heart, to sarcastic and cynical commentaries on contemporary Israeli society.

Israelis have also made a mark in film. The Israeli film industry began in the 1950s, with notable films focusing on the heroism of the early Israelis such as *Hill 24 Does Not Answer* and *They Were Ten.* As the industry matured, it began producing films dealing with the complexities of modern life in Israel and how the Holocaust has affected survivors and their children; Gila Almagor's *The Summer of Aviya* and the sequel *Under the Domin Tree* are good examples of the second category. *Shu'ur* by Hannah Azoulai and Shmuel Hasfari and *Coffee with Lemon* by Leonid Govirets focus on the problems of new immigrants. Films by other directors have addressed the Arab–Israeli conflict and the difficulties facing women in Israeli society. The film industry received a boost and a nod of recognition in recent years when Jewish American director Steven

✡ HEBREW BOOK WEEK

Israelis are a nation of readers. They buy more than 11 million books per year, putting them on par with the two other top reading nations in the world, Sweden and Iceland. Considering the tiny size of Israel and its population of only 6 million, the fact that there are over two thousand publishing companies in Israel putting out over four thousand titles a year (more than ten per day) is testimony to Israelis' love of reading. Across the nation, in more than a dozen cities and forty smaller towns, an event known as Hebrew Book Week has been held each June since 1961. It is estimated that around half the Israeli population goes to the book fairs that are the centerpiece of the event. There, publishers display and sell books, primarily in Hebrew but occasionally in Arabic or Russian, to a population eager for the opportunities for growth and entertainment that books represent.

Spielberg established the Spielberg Film Archive at Hebrew University in Jerusalem. The goal is to preserve all Israeli films as well as all other world films dealing with Jewish subject matter.

MUSIC

The development of Israeli music followed much the same path as the visual arts, literature, and film: It had its beginnings in the artistic traditions and values of the immigrant cultures that make up the nation but eventually forged something uniquely Israeli. In fact, most Israelis would probably agree that, of all the arts, it is in their music that their national spirit and identity is most widely and profoundly expressed.

The ability to express oneself musically and to participate in the community through dancing, singing, and playing a musical instrument has always been a central part of Jewish identity. In fact, musical ability was so widespread among European Jewish immigrants that a joke arose that, when a new group of immigrants disembarked, those not carrying violins, flutes, clarinets, and the like could be assumed to play the piano. In the 1930s, with the rise of the Nazi Party in Germany, many highly educated, middle-class Jews left Europe for Palestine. Upon their arrival they began to set up symphony and chamber music orchestras and other musical institutions. In the 1990s, the influx of nearly a quarter-million Russian Jews added immeasurably to the depth of musical talent in the nation. These immigrants have enhanced the quality of the already renowned Israeli Philharmonic Orchestra and New Israel Opera in Tel Aviv and have provided opportunities for talented young Israelis to take music lessons and study at music conservatories staffed by some of the highest-quality teachers in the world.

Composers developed a distinctly Israeli style of music, following a similar path to that of the visual artists. They initially followed primarily European styles, then branched out in subsequent generations to incorporate Jewish themes from religious observances and a wide variety of folk traditions. Some composers, including Mordechai Seter, developed what became known as the Mediterranean style, using the rhythms and melodic styles of Yemeni and other Middle Eastern Jews, Eastern Mediterranean musical traditions, and Jewish religious music. Paul Ben-Haim, Oedon Partos, and

A DREAM OF PEACE

One of the most renowned Israeli musical stars today is Naomi Shemer. Even in a country whose popular songs commonly have sensitive lyrics, Shemer's songs stand out for their exceptional poetry. Her song "Jerusalem of Gold" is, to many, the unofficial second national anthem of Israel, with its beautiful chorus, "Oh Jerusalem of gold and of light and of bronze / I am the lute for all your songs." In this song, "Let It Be" (translated from the website "Fifty Years of Hebrew Song"), Shemer expresses her vision of more peaceful times.

There's still a white sail brave and gleaming, though the skies are black and low Everything we wish, let it be. And when at evening by the window, Sabbath candles softly glow Everything we wish, let it be.

I hear the sound of people singing, bugle notes that fill the air Everything we wish, let it be. Above the fanfare and the music, let them hear my silent prayer Everything we wish, let it be.

Within a green and quiet village stands a house with open door Everything we wish, let it be. The summer's ended, and the journey. Bring the soldiers home once more. Everything we wish, let it be.

And when a distant star from heaven lights our darkness from above Everything we wish, let it be.

Oh, give them strength and give them quiet, those we cherish, those we love Everything we wish, let it be.

Let it be, let it be Only let it be Everything we wish, let it be.

Alexander Uriah Boscovitch are among the composers who pioneered this uniquely Israeli classical music.

As important as classical music may be to Israeli culture, it has not had nearly the influence on typical Israelis that popular and folk music have had. Israel has an exciting popular music scene. Possibly because most Israeli pop stars sing in Hebrew, a language that is not even universally familiar to the 2 percent of the world's population who is Jewish, many have not achieved the international recognition they deserve. Many major stars today have been popular in Israel for many years, including Chava Albertsein, Shalom

Hanoch, Corinne Allal, Naomi Shemer, Shlomo Artzi, David Broza, Arik Einstein, an artist known simply as Rita, and Rita's husband, Rami Kleinstein. In addition to solo performers, Israel has a number of excellent bands, including Tipex, Gaia, Sheva, and HaChaverim Shel Natasha.

Israeli popular music styles range from simple and sweet to loud and energetic. But what most typifies the kind of music heard on the radio is a very melodic song performed by an artist with a beautiful voice, backed up by fairly simple accompaniment so that the poetic words and ideas in the lyrics can be appreciated. Life in Israel is difficult, and Israelis cannot avoid being touched by the violence that surrounds them, or being troubled by the moral contradictions in their society between what should be and what is. So, even popular songs tend to deal with serious issues, and more superficial songs rarely get much airtime. In many songs, the bittersweetness of life and the complexities of finding one's way through difficult times are woven in with universal themes of love not just for another person but for family and country. Hope, joy, fear, sorrow, and the whole range of human emotions are exposed and celebrated in Israeli music. It and all the art forms of Israel are ways Israelis convey to each other and to the world their unique spirit born of their complex history, culture, religious heritage, and sense of national destiny, a spirit that continues to energize this tiny but truly extraordinary nation.

Israel Faces
the Future

"Ask two Jews their opinion and you will get three answers."
This common saying among Jews is a reflection of the love
for intellectual debate that has been at the heart of Jewish
culture for millennia. Though Israelis share this love of ar-
gument, if one were to ask the nearly 5 million Jews of Israel
today to name the biggest issue affecting their nation, it is
likely there would be only one answer: the conflict between
the Arab world and Israel, or, more specifically, the problem
of coexistence with the Palestinian Arabs. As easy as it
might be to think of nothing else in modern-day Israel,
there are nevertheless many other important issues facing
the nation. Some are part of the ripple effect from the inse-
curity caused by the Arab–Israeli conflict, and some would
exist even if that were resolved. Israel has many strengths to
draw on, including the resilience and commitment of its
people, as well as a history of a stable democratic process
that provides the framework for decision making and problem solving. "This country has everything—except peace,"[26]
one middle-aged Israeli woman recently remarked, echo-
ing the sentiments of many of her fellow Israelis. Even
though the present is a time of despair and confusion for
many Israelis, there is little reason to doubt that if peace
can be achieved—admittedly a big if—a strong and vibrant
national future will follow.

Living with the Palestinians

Beyond the basic agreement about their country's biggest problem, Israelis are deeply divided about how to resolve it. Some
feel that an independent nation of Palestine is deserved and
should be immediately established. Others think it should not
be established until Palestinian leadership gets control of terrorist groups. Still others say that a Palestinian state should be
set up elsewhere, outside of Israeli territory.

There are several related issues about which Israelis are deeply divided and these have consistently hampered peace talks and negotiations. One issue is the future of the settlements. Some Israelis argue that the land is legitimately theirs and settlements should go forward vigorously. Others, however, see a growing Israeli presence on the West Bank as disrespectful to the Palestinian dream for their own homeland. Another related issue is the deployment of the military in the Palestinian territories. Some argue that military force is the only way terrorism can be suppressed right now, but others say that it makes long-range solutions more difficult to achieve because it antagonizes Palestinians even more. Yet another issue is the status of Jerusalem. Both sides want the city as the capital of their state and seem unable to concede it for any amount of peace or land.

A CYCLE OF MISTRUST

Though Israelis let themselves hope a little whenever there seems to be movement toward peace, few have much confidence in international conferences, diplomatic missions, or peace talks. Both Palestinians and Israelis believe the other side is insincere about wanting peace, and both think the opposing side is unwilling to give up anything to those perceived as enemies. Several recent attempts to reach a settlement leading to a Palestinian homeland have broken down. In 1999, Israeli prime minister Ehud Barak offered the Palestinians almost all the land they asked for and Arafat appeared ready to agree, until he suddenly and unexpectedly changed his mind. The Bush administration had gotten discussions back under way in 2002 when a new spate of suicide bombings caused Israeli prime minister Ariel Sharon to order tanks into West Bank cities, effectively ending any chance for continued talks.

The essential problem is that Israel is being asked to give up land for peace. It has shown its willingness to do this in the past, and many believe that such a step is inevitable in the future. However, Israelis have little confidence that giving up land now will actually bring peace. There is deep doubt of Arafat's ability, or indeed his true willingness, to control terrorism against Israeli citizens. Documentary evidence has shown that Arafat's Palestinian Authority has financially supported violent groups such as the Al Aqsa Martyrs Brigade, which has carried out a number of suicide bombings in Israel. Therefore, the peace process is hampered by the necessity of working with a leader in whom Israel has no confidence to accomplish a task most likely beyond his control.

If Israel gave up the West Bank, with its long open border, it could easily find that the new sovereign nation of Palestine had no intention of controlling terrorist groups. Worse, any sovereign nation can set up its own army and arsenal of weapons, as well as declare war and choose its allies. The nation of Palestine could cross its border and reach almost every Israeli town and city within a matter of hours or, in some cases, minutes. If it allied militarily with Iraq, which has in the past sent SCUD missiles into Israel from bases inside Iraq and has made its desire to destroy Israel very clear, Israel could indeed be unable to withstand the assault. For many Israelis, these seem like very real prospects that can be avoided simply by putting off or rejecting altogether the idea of a Palestinian state in the West Bank.

However, major world leaders such as U.S. president George W. Bush have put extreme pressure on Israel to end its military occupation of the West Bank and rectify the living conditions and civil rights of Palestinians living in the territories. World opinion favors an independent Palestine, and Israeli prime minister Sharon has found himself in the same position as others before him. He is forced to agree in principle with the idea of a Palestinian state, and at least appear to be open to working toward that goal, while believing that the conditions are not yet right for any real progress toward it. For the time being,

✡ SECURITY, ISRAELI STYLE

The line of cars forms down the block from the single entrance to the shopping mall. An armed security guard looks into the face of every person in each car and asks the driver to pop the trunk latch. After a quick look in the trunk and the passenger compartment, and occasionally a check of identity, the car moves on. In some malls, additional guards scan the parking lot from watchtowers. At the entrance to the mall, people put their bags and purses down on a table for another guard to search and then lift their arms for the metal-detecting wand. Inside the mall, other armed guards are visible, and some major stores have their own security to make one final check of anyone going inside.

This is life in Israel today. Although deadly bombings are nothing new, and unattended packages have been routinely blown up for years by explosives specialists known as sappers, in recent times watchfulness has greatly increased as a result of a number of suicide bombings inside public places. Such measures have been extremely successful, as have Israeli intelligence efforts to stop bombers before they reach their destination. Still, such efforts do not stop bombings entirely. In one recent event, a bomber who realized that she would not get past security at the Mahane Yehuda vegetable market in Jerusalem simply walked to the nearby bus stop and blew herself up there. In another incident, bombers did not even try to board a bus but instead pulled up alongside and in a massive detonation blew up the car and the bus. It is not likely that security measures will prevent all suicide bombings, but they have allowed a greater sense of normalcy in Israeli life at a very difficult time.

Israel's emphasis has been on changing Palestinian leadership and creating a more smoothly functioning and less corrupt government as a precondition for further talks.

THE ECONOMY

If indeed peace can be achieved, Israel is likely to have a bright future. However, its present economic situation also seriously jeopardizes that future. The latest Intifada has left the country reeling. Tourism, a $3 billion a year industry in good times, has been almost completely destroyed by fear of suicide bombers. Despite Israeli efforts to encourage travel, it is estimated to have dropped by as much as 90 percent over the last few years. Tour operators, hotels, restaurants, artisan workshops, and all those who depend on tourist spending have felt the pinch. Other businesses have felt the chilling effect as well with the rise in unemployment. Declines in global high-tech industries, one of Israel's strongest economic bases, have only made things worse. And large call-ups of military reservists bring business near a standstill.

The fear of a difficult economic future makes Israelis cautious about spending what little discretionary money they have. Those who set aside their fears of bombers to go shopping at local malls are buying less, and thus the overall economy continues to decline. The best indicator of this is the fall in value of the Israeli currency, the shekel, which has dropped in the last several years from three to the dollar to five to the dollar, dropping a half a shekel in the first few months of 2002 alone. New economic programs introduced by the Sharon government in mid-2002 stressed cutbacks in government services and support and increases in many taxes at a time when the typical Israeli is already in difficult economic shape.

IMMIGRATION

Further straining the ability of Israel to take care of its people is the increase in immigration. In the last decade, hundreds of thousands of immigrants have made aliyah, the Hebrew term for immigrating to Israel, with Russians and North Africans making up the majority of immigrants. Because of the downturn in the economy, many immigrants have trouble finding

Israeli soldiers guard a checkpoint near Gaza.

jobs. Sociologists and political scientists have spoken out with increasing concern about the consequences of this. Long-term unemployment is the first step in the creation of a chronically poor lower class. Though there are discrepancies in income between Israelis, class differences between rich and poor have been less noticeable than in many other countries, including the United States.

To date, the poorest Israelis have been primarily the newest immigrants, but in general they quickly moved into the middle class once they mastered the language and either trained for a new career or found a job related to their previous training, education, and experience. This no longer seems to be true. Israel, for example, already has more doctors and other medical personnel than any other country its size, and there is little unmet demand for other skills such as the ability to teach music or foreign languages. Many middle-aged Russian immigrants, for example, had professions in Russia, but today they guard the entrances to shopping malls in Israel because there is no better work to be found. Sadly, those jobs always seem to be plentiful and available; nearly every place people congregate is now guarded.

DIFFERENT KINDS OF JEWS

At the heart of many of the dilemmas facing Israel today is an often-quarrelsome legislature that is deeply divided over many critical issues other than the Palestinian problem and the economy. One of these issues is the role of Judaism in Israel. There is little doubt that the idea of a Jewish homeland has been realized. In the center of the Israeli flag is a Star of David, one of the symbols of Judaism, and Israeli citizenship is considered a birthright of every Jew in the world who wishes to exercise it by coming to live in the country. It is the only place in the world where Jews are not a minority, and the only place in the world where they can invoke their religious beliefs and practices as the foundation for a national way of life.

Yet to conclude from this that Israeli life is centered around the practice of Judaism would be a mistake. Israelis are quick to point out that the array of terms for different kinds of American Jews—Reform, Conservative, Modern Orthodox, Reconstructionist, and so on—have no meaning in Israel. "In Israel there are only two kinds of Jews: religious and nonreligious,"[27] a longtime resident of Jerusalem explains, and the distance between the two types is great. The most strongly felt religious animosity in Israel is not between Jews and Israeli Muslims but between secular Jews and ultra-Orthodox ones. Haredi leaders continually assail the rest of the population for having betrayed the covenant at the core of Judaism; many nonreligious Israelis, on the other hand, look at the Haredi as wrapped up in their own world and working at odds with the needs of the country.

A FRACTURED POLITICAL SYSTEM

The divisiveness surrounding these and other issues makes taking any consistent and sustained government action difficult. Israelis directly elect their prime minister, but the Knesset is selected based on the overall number of votes a particular party receives. There are several dozen parties in

---

✡ THE ULTRA-ORTHODOX

In Israel, religious intolerance rarely occurs between faiths. Nevertheless, it is rampant between secular Jews and ultra-Orthodox, or Hasidic, Jews. To the ultra-Orthodox, there is only one way to practice Judaism, the way laid down in the Torah. Being less than absolutely observant puts one outside of the covenant with God and thus outside the religion altogether. In fact, ultra-Orthodox rabbis have announced publicly that a Jewish couple married by a Reform rabbi might as well have been married by a Catholic priest, and that non-Orthodox Jews should not be treated as Jews at all for the purpose of immigration to Israel. Their council of rabbis very openly calls other Jews insulting names, and incidents have been reported of female visitors to ultra-Orthodox neighborhoods being spat on because their shoulders or legs were bare.

Typically, ultra-Orthodox Jews live in their own neighborhoods, operate their own shops and businesses, attend their own schools, and avoid involvement with others as much as possible. Ultra-Orthodox Jews believe that a person's most sacred duty is life-long study of the Torah. This is a major cause of resentment in Israel today, because those who choose not to work a regular job but simply devote their lives to studying the Torah are financially supported by yeshivas, but yeshivas are largely supported by tax dollars. Hence, Israelis foot the bill for the lives of study of people who despise them. The ultra-Orthodox have also been able to use their political clout to establish state subsidies for families with more than five children, so taxpayers also foot the bill for what are generally large ultra-Orthodox families. Added to many Israelis' resentment is the fact that ultra-Orthodox youth do not serve in the military. To the typical Israeli, there is something hypocritical about living off the money and accepting the protection of people they openly revile in a country they do not defend.

Israel, most of which have only a few seats in the Knesset, and though one might think this would make them limited in their power, the opposite is sometimes the case.

Candidates run for prime minister as members of a party. Then the candidate receiving the most votes is given the opportunity to set up a government. However, his or her party typically holds only about 20 percent of the seats in the Knesset, so the new prime minister has to bring other parties into a coalition to create the majority required. Thus, small groups organized around single issues, such as strengthening the settlements or preserving Jewish law, must be courted by the prime minister. They find themselves in a position to influence government policy far beyond what their numbers in the population would really warrant by demanding cabinet and ministry posts and concessions on their key issues.

As a result, the prime minister rarely has much deep support in the Knesset or even among his or her own cabinet.

Commonly during times of crisis, a cabinet minister or a party will threaten to leave the government, potentially upsetting the coalition. The prime minister, therefore, puts enormous amounts of time and energy into making sure he or she has a majority, rather than forming and carrying out consistent policies and programs. Because Israel does not have set election days (it has an outside limit of four years before new elections for prime minister must be held), any loss of confidence in the prime minister could result in a breakdown of the coalition and a call for an early election to choose a new prime minister. The last two prime ministers, Benjamin Netanyahu and Ehud Barak, both lost their jobs when their coalitions collapsed only partway into their terms in office. So far, Ariel Sharon, despite deeply divided sentiments among his cabinet over such things as ways to stimulate the economy and combat terrorism, has been able to keep his coalition together. But some surprising recent statements about the inevitability of a Palestinian state have alienated many, even in his own Likud Party, and his steps to revive the Israeli economy have been widely criticized.

As a result of the nearly constant shift in policies and priorities, many important issues that need to be addressed, such as health care, education, energy and water conservation, and improved national transportation systems, do not get the sustained attention and focus they require. The situation may be helped a little by the recent decision to have the Knesset elect the prime minister after the next Knesset elections in 2003,

Israeli Prime Minister Ariel Sharon (far right) and other cabinet ministers vote for emergency economic measures in the Knesset in May 2002.

A TURNING POINT IN ISRAELI HISTORY: THE NETANYA MASSACRE

On March 27, 2002, 250 guests were arriving to begin the celebration of Passover at the Park Hotel in Netanya, a coastal resort city north of Tel Aviv. Jews commemorate Passover, one of their most important holidays, with a special meal known as the Seder, complete with special rituals, symbolic foods, and holiday songs. Passover commemorates the release of the Hebrews from slavery in Egypt, and the celebration begins with the question, "Why is this night unlike all other nights?" Ironically, shortly before that question would have been asked, it was answered by a massive explosion at the entry to the dining room. A Palestinian from the West Bank town of Tulkarem, less than ten miles away, had blown himself up at the entry to the dining room. Twenty-nine people were killed, including six elderly survivors of the Holocaust, and 140 were injured. Both Hamas and Al Aqsa Martyrs Brigade claimed responsibility for the bombing. It was the highest casualty toll of any civilian attack since the beginning of the Second Intifada almost two years before, and because it came on such a holy night, it was instantly perceived as one of the worst things that had ever happened in Israel.

Lydia Lanxner, a nurse at a Netanya hospital, did not realize until later that a woman who died in her care was a good friend because she had been so severely mangled. Later, Lanxner put the meaning of Netanya for Israelis in perspective (quoted by Laura King in the story "Passover Attack Memories Still Fresh"): "To me, and to many people I know, this attack, coming at the time it did, at the beginning of this particular holiday, put it in the real context of our nationhood, of our ability to survive as a people. How could it not?"

For more than a week before the Netanya massacre, the Sharon government, despite heavy criticism, had not responded to several other suicide bombings as a way of showing the world that Israel was serious about pursuing peace negotiations. Nearly daily, stories of both successful and unsuccessful bombers had been filling the news. One person had been caught wearing an explosive-packed vest while riding in a Palestinian ambulance, purportedly taking a patient to an Israeli hospital. Another blew himself up inside his car when he was approached for a routine check outside a Jerusalem shopping mall.

Respecting an agreement that the Palestinian Authority make all arrests in its own territory, Israel had waited, for months and sometimes years, for suspected terrorists it wanted to question and perhaps detain to be arrested, but few arrests were made. The bomber at Netanya had been on the list of suspected terrorists for several years. After the incident at Netanya, Israel decided to move in and take care of the matter itself. Within a few days, the Israeli reserves had been called up and West Bank cities were surrounded by tanks and searched by Israeli soldiers. It was the largest Israeli military operation in several decades, and included the controversial sieges of Yasser Arafat's compound in Ramallah, the Jenin refugee camp, and the Church of the Nativity in Bethlehem.

rather than having candidates run in a general election. But the real problem is the number of small parties that make uneasy coalitions a fact of life in Israeli politics.

THE WILL TO SURVIVE

Despite the problems diversity causes, it is also one of Israel's greatest strengths. Immigrants who longed for years to make aliyah remind more jaded Israelis of how precious a thing their country is. The ultra-Orthodox are frowned upon by many Israelis because they do not serve in the military or hold paying jobs; they receive state stipends simply to engage in a life of study and strict religious observance. However, even many of those who resent the use of their taxes for this purpose will begrudgingly admit that the strength, and perhaps even the existence, of Judaism today must at least in part be attributed to the unflagging efforts of extremely observant Jews over the centuries.

But for typical Israelis, Jewishness is simply a given, a trait so common in Israel that it disappears into the background. This is not to say that being Jewish does not matter to Israelis—far from it. They are well aware of how anti-Semitism has impacted both their past and their present, and though they may ignore most events on the Jewish religious calendar and seek out places to buy bread during Passover and groceries on Shabbat, they do so as Jews who have exercised their right not to practice their faith but nevertheless be part of a people and a nation.

Newcomers and tourists often express amazement that nearly everywhere in Israel, whether one is sunning on the beach, picking vegetables in the market, or strolling through a mall, almost every person one sees is a Jew. They may be jet-black and wearing the bright colors of their native Ethiopia or sunburned and blue-eyed South African immigrants. They may be thin and dark like their Moroccan ancestors or broad shouldered and tall like their Russian ones. They may be covered from head to foot or wear only a postage-stamp-sized bikini. Their heads may sport a yarmulke, an army beret, headphones, a large black hat, a baseball cap, or nothing at all. They may carry a prayer book, a cell phone, or a designer handbag. However they look, wherever they came from, and whatever their views, they come together to form one people, the Jews, and one nation, the Israelis.

FACTS ABOUT ISRAEL

GEOGRAPHY

Area: 12,706 square miles, slightly smaller than New Jersey

Border countries: Egypt, Jordan, Lebanon, and Syria

Climate: Temperate along the coast; hot and dry in the deserts

Terrain: Desert in the south; low coastal plains; central mountains; and the Jordan rift valley in the east

Elevation extremes: Dead Sea:–1,300 feet

   Har Meron: 3,955 feet

Natural resources: Timber, potash, copper ore, natural gas, phosphate rock, magnesium bromide, clays, sand, and oil

Land use: Arable land: 17%; Permanent crops: 4%; Permanent pastures: 7%; Forests and woodlands: 6%; Other: 66%

Geography note: There are 231 settlements and land use sites in the West Bank; 42 in the Golan Heights; 25 in the Gaza Strip; and 2 in East Jerusalem.

PEOPLE

Population: 5,938,093 (July 2001 estimate)

Note: Includes 176,000 settlers in the West Bank, 20,000 in the Golan Heights, 6,900 in the Gaza Strip, and 173,000 in East Jerusalem.

Age structure: 0–14 years: 27.36%; 15–64 years: 62.73%; 65+ years: 9.91%

Population growth: 1.58%

Birth rate: 19.12 births/1,000 population

Death rate: 6.22 deaths/1,000 population

Net migration rate: 2.85 migrants/1,000 population

Infant mortality rate: 7.72 deaths/1,000 live births

Life expectancy at birth: 78.71 years

   Male: 76.69 years

   Female: 80.84 years

Total fertility rate: 2.57 children born per woman

Ethnic groups: Jewish: 80.1% (Europe/America born, 32.1%; Israel born, 20.8%; Africa born, 14.6%; Asia born, 12.6%;)

   Non-Jewish: 19.9%;

Religions: Jewish: 80.1%; Muslim: 14.6%; Christian: 2.1%; Other: 3.2%

Languages: Hebrew (the official national language), Arabic, and English (the most common foreign language)

Literacy (age 15 and over who can read and write): 95%

GOVERNMENT

Government type: Parliamentary democracy

Capital: Jerusalem

Note: Israel proclaimed Jerusalem its capital in 1950, but the U.S. and most other embassies are in Tel Aviv.

Administrative divisions: Central, Haifa, Jerusalem, Northern, Southern, and Tel Aviv

Date of independence: May 14, 1948

Note: Independence Day falls on the 5th of Iyar of the Jewish lunar calendar, so the celebration only occasionally falls on May 14.

Constitution: No formal constitution. Some foundational documents serve in this role to a certain extent, including the Declaration of Establishment (1948), the Basic Laws of the Knesset, and the Israeli citizenship law.

Legal system: Mixture of English common law and, in personal matters, religious legal systems

Voting age: 18

Executive branch:

Chief of state: President Moshe Katsav (since 2000)

Note: This is a Knesset-elected post that has only a limited oversight role.

Head of government: Prime Minister Ariel Sharon (since 2001)

Cabinet: Selected by prime minister and approved by Knesset

Elections: The president is elected by the Knesset for a five-year term (the last election held was in July 2000); the prime minister is elected by popular vote for a four-year term (last election held in February 2001)

Note: In 2003, Israel will return to its former system of having the Knesset elect the prime minister.

Legislative branch:

Unicameral (one-house) Knesset: 120 seats; members elected by popular vote to four-year terms

Note: All parties receiving more than 1% of the popular vote are represented.

MAY 1999 ELECTIONS

Results:	Percent	Seats
One Israel	20.0%	26
Likud	14.1%	19
Shas	13.0%	17
MERETZ	7.6%	10
Yisra'el Ba'Aliya	5.1%	6
Shinui	5.0%	6
Center Party	5.0%	6
National Religious	4.2%	5
United Torah Judaism	3.7%	5
United Arab List	3.4%	5

Results:	Percent	Seats
National Union	3.0%	4
Hadash	2.6%	3
Yisr'el Beteinu	2.6%	4
Balad	1.9%	2
One Nation	1.9%	2
Other	6.9%	0

Note: Gush Emunim and Peace Now are opposing political pressure groups not functioning as political parties. Gush Emunim advocates Jewish settlement on the West Bank and Peace Now supports territorial concessions.

Judicial branch: Supreme court (justices are appointed for life by the president)

ECONOMY (FIGURES FOR YEAR 2000)

Overview: Israel has an advance market economy using high technology. There is substantial government support for private industry. Israel depends on imports of oil, grains, raw materials, and military equipment. Despite very limited amounts of arable land, it has intensively developed agriculture and, except for grain, is self-sufficient agriculturally. Cut diamonds, high-tech equipment, and agricultural products are the main exports, but Israel has a trade deficit. Roughly half of the country's debt is to the United States, which provides over $1 billion a year in aid. Israel's population grew by one-sixth as a result of recent immigration, primarily of Jews from the former Soviet Union, who brought skills that will be useful in Israel's future economic growth. Growth was a strong 5.9%; in 2000, but the new Intifada devastated tourism, and this, coupled with a slowdown in high-tech industries, slowed economic growth to 2%; in 2001, and further losses are anticipated.

Gross domestic product (GDP)/purchasing power: $110.2 billion

GDP per capita: $18,900

GDP by sector: Agriculture: 4%; Industry: 37%; Services: 59%

Labor force: 2.4 million

Labor force by occupation: Public services: 31.2%; Manufacturing: 20.2%; Finance and business: 13.1%; Commerce: 12.8%; Construction: 7.5%; Agriculture, forestry, and fishing: 2.6%; Other: 12.6%;

Unemployment rate: 9%

Budget: Revenues: $40 billion

Expenditures: $42.4 billion

Industries: High-technology products (aviation, communications, computer-aided design and manufacturing, medical electronics), wood and paper products, potash and phosphates, food, beverages, tobacco, and diamond cutting

Agriculture: Citrus, vegetables, cotton, beef, poultry, and dairy products

Exports: $31.5 billion (machinery and equipment, software, cut diamonds, agricultural products, chemicals, textiles, and clothing)

Imports: $35.1 billion (raw materials, military equipment, rough diamonds, fuels, and consumer goods)

External debt: $38 billion

Currency: New Israeli shekel (NIS)

Exchange value in mid-2002: 5 shekels=$1

Note: The shekel has devalued against the dollar since 1996, when the shekel traded at 3 to the dollar. In 2000 the shekel traded at 4 to the dollar. This is an indication of a depressed economic environment in Israel today.

COMMUNICATIONS

Cellular telephones in use: 2.5 million

Main-line telephones in use: 2.8 million

Televisions: 1.7 million

Internet users: 1 million

MILITARY

Israel Defense Forces (IDF): Ground, naval, and air components

Military service age: 18

Military manpower availability (ages 15–49):

Males: 1,522,000

Females: 1,482,000

Military manpower reaching military age annually:

Males: 49,200

Females: 53,400

Military expenditures: $8.7 billion

Military as percent of GDP: 9.4%

NOTES

CHAPTER 1: HA'ARETZ: THE LAND

1. Pam Barrett, ed., *Insight Guide: Israel.* New York: Langenscheidt, 2000, p. 195.

2. Barrett, *Insight Guide: Israel,* p. 198.

3. Barrett, *Insight Guide: Israel,* p. 256.

CHAPTER 2: A VISION IN THE DESERT: THE CREATION OF A JEWISH HOMELAND

4. Benny Morris, *Righteous Victims: A History of the Zionist-Arab Conflict, 1881–2001.* New York: Vintage Books, 2001, p. 49.

5. Quoted in George Robinson, *Essential Judaism: A Complete Guide to Beliefs, Customs, and Rituals.* New York: Pocket Books, 2000, p. 537.

6. Quoted in Morris, *Righteous Victims,* p. 90.

7. Quoted in Morris, *Righteous Victims,* p. 91.

8. Quoted in Morris, *Righteous Victims,* p. 91.

9. Quoted in Morris, *Righteous Victims,* p. 94.

10. Morris, *Righteous Victims,* p. 100.

11. Morris, *Righteous Victims,* p. 129.

12. Daniel Jacobs, *Israel and the Palestinian Territories: The Rough Guide.* London: Rough Guides, 1998, p. 492.

CHAPTER 3: PROMISES TO KEEP: BUILDING A JEWISH NATION

13. Quoted in Robinson, *Essential Judaism,* p. 539.

14. Avi Shlaim, *The Iron Wall: Israel and the Arab World.* New York: W.W. Norton, 2001, p. 36.

15. Raymond P. Scheindlin, *A Short History of the Jewish People.* Oxford, England: Oxford University Press, 1998, p. 237.

16. Shlaim, *The Iron Wall,* p. 241.

17. Quoted in Jacobs, *Israel,* p. 496.

18. Shlaim, *The Iron Wall*, p. 320.

19. Shlaim, *The Iron Wall*, p. 320.

20. Morris, *Righteous Victims*, p. 547.

CHAPTER 4: BUILDING UP AND BREAKING DOWN: THE STRUGGLE FOR PEACE AND PROSPERITY

21. Quoted in Shlaim, *The Iron Wall*, p. 316.

22. Quoted in Morris, *Righteous Victims*, p. 635.

23. Quoted in Ahron Bregman and Jihan El-Tahri, *Israel and the Arabs*. New York: TV Books, 2000, p. 340.

24. Bregman and El-Tahri, *Israel and the Arabs*, p. 339.

CHAPTER 6: COMMON ROOTS AND CREATIVE VISIONS: ARTS AND CULTURE IN ISRAEL

25. Quoted in "Tannenbaum Tourist Center: The Chagall Windows" (brochure). Jerusalem: Hadassah Hebrew University Medical Center, 2000.

CHAPTER 7: ISRAEL FACES THE FUTURE

26. Shoshanna Reichl, interview with the author, June 12, 2002.

27. David Frank, interview with the author, March 23, 2002.

GLOSSARY

aliyah: A Hebrew word referring to Jewish immigration to Israel.

annex: To incorporate a territory into another country without conquering it militarily.

anti-Semitism: Hostility toward or discrimination against Jews or Judaism.

civilian: Nonmilitary.

coalition: An agreement by different groups to work together to increase their influence and power; a government formed by pulling together a number of parties to create a majority.

Cold War: The commonly used name for the roughly fifty-year period of conflict between the Soviet Union and the United States.

covenant: A term used in Judaism to refer to the pact made between God and the Jews that they would follow his rules in exchange for his protection.

Diaspora: The dispersal of Jewish people away from their homeland.

Holocaust: The deliberate and systematic attempt to murder the world's Jews by the Nazis in World War II; often called HaShoah by the Jews.

Jewish mysticism: A form of Judaism focusing on the direct experience of God as well as the study of the complex patterns in nature and the physical universe.

kibbutz: A community that works collectively and shares the proceeds of their labor; the term is used exclusively in Israel.

kosher: From the Hebrew "kashruth," a term used to describe food that is permissible under the laws laid down in the Torah.

mandate: An arrangement in which a powerful nation

serves as the temporary governor of another nation for the purpose of preparing it for eventual independence and self-rule.

mufti: A jurist who interprets Islamic law; applied as an honorary title to the Muslim political leader of Jerusalem at the time of the British mandate.

pogrom: A campaign of terrorism, destruction, and physical violence against Jews in eastern Europe in the nineteenth and twentieth centuries.

rabbi: A Jewish spiritual leader.

scroll: Something written on one long sheet of material, such as sheepskin or paper, which is then rolled up and read by unrolling rather than turning pages.

secular: Nonreligious.

siege: Trapping people inside a confined space and then waiting until they are forced to surrender by hunger, thirst, or other emergencies.

tel: A mound formed over the centuries by cities building new structures over the ruins of the old.

wadi: A dry desert streambed filled with water only after rainstorms.

Zionism: The movement to establish a Jewish homeland at the site of the biblical "Promised Land."

CHRONOLOGY

1881
Eliezer Ben-Yehuda moves to Jerusalem and raises his child to speak only Hebrew, establishing the practicality of Hebrew as a living language.

1882
The first Jewish settlement in Palestine, Rishon le Tsiyon, is established.

1895
Theodor Herzl covers the Alfred Dreyfus trial and formulates the idea of Zionism.

1897
The first Zionist conference is held in Switzerland; the World Zionist Organization is established.

1901
The Jewish National Fund is set up to buy land in Palestine.

1909
Tel Aviv is founded; the first kibbutz at Deganya is founded.

1917
The Balfour Declaration announces British government support for a Jewish homeland in Palestine.

1918
Britain is given a mandate over Palestine.

1920
A deadly Arab riot in Jerusalem kills several hundred, mostly Jews.

1921
A deadly Arab riot in Jaffa kills several hundred Arabs and Jews; Haj Amin al-Husseini is named mufti of Jerusalem.

1936
The Palestinian Revolt results in strikes and sabotage across Palestine; al-Husseini is removed as mufti.

1939
The British White Paper seeks to limit Jewish immigration to Palestine to placate Arabs.

1939–1945
World War II and the Holocaust occur.

1946
An explosion at King David Hotel kills ninety-one British and others.

1947
The United Nations agrees to partition Palestine into Arab and Jewish sections.

1948
The massacre at Deir Yassin occurs; the British mandate ends; the State of Israel is established; the War of Independence occurs.

1950
The Absentee Property Act confiscates Arab property in Israel; the Law of Return grants the right of automatic citizenship to all Jews immigrating to Israel; David Ben-Gurion becomes Israel's first prime minister.

1956
The war with Egypt occurs; Israel captures and then gives back the Sinai Peninsula.

1957
The draining of the Hula Valley is completed and first communities established.

1967
The Six Day War occurs, Israel captures the West Bank, the Golan Heights, and the Gaza Strip and reclaims western Jerusalem, thus establishing its current national borders.

1970
The PLO tries to overthrow the government of Jordan and is expelled to Lebanon.

1972
Palestinian terrorists kill Israeli athletes at the Munich Olympics.

1973
The Yom Kippur War occurs.

1976
The rescue of hostages at Entebbe shows Israel's ability to carry out counterterrorism.

1977
Egyptian president Anwar Sadat addresses Knesset on his plan for peace.

1979
The Camp David Accords by Sadat and Israeli prime minister Menachem Begin provide for the Israeli withdrawal from the Sinai in exchange for peace with Egypt.

1982–1985
The war with Lebanon occurs over PLO incursions into Israel.

1984
Operation Moses rescues fifteen thousand Ethiopian Jews from refugee camps in Sudan.

1987
The first Palestinian Intifada occurs.

1989
Operation Exodus brings 700,000 Soviet Jews to Israel.

1991
The Gulf War takes place, Iraqi SCUD missiles are fired into Israel; the Madrid peace talks occur; Operation Solomon rescues twenty thousand Ethiopian Jews.

1992
Yitzhak Rabin is elected prime minister.

1993
The Oslo Accords are announced, outlining a declaration of principles for reaching a lasting peace between Israelis and Palestinians.

1995
Rabin is assassinated.

1996
Benjamin Netanyahu is elected prime minister.

1999
Ehud Barak is elected prime minister.

2000
The second Intifada is declared.

2001
Ariel Sharon is elected prime minister.

2002
A suicide bombing on Passover prompts the IDF reoccupation of the West Bank.

FOR FURTHER READING

BOOKS

Mary Jane Cahill, *Israel*. New York: Chelsea House, 1997. Good basic information about Israel's history, geography, and people.

Larry Collins and Dominique LaPierre, *O Jerusalem*. New York: Simon & Schuster, 1988. This exciting and dramatic version of the story of the siege of Jerusalem and surrounding events reads like a novel.

Nathaniel Harris, *Israel and Arab Nations in Conflict*. New York: Raintree/Steck Vaughan, 1999. Very good discussion of the origins and consequences of the strife between Arabs and Israelis.

Laurel Holliday, *Children of Israel, Children of Palestine: Our Own True Stories*. New York: Pocket Books, 1999. A collection of memoirs by children growing up in Israel from 1948 on.

Arlene Kurtis and Jona Lerman, *Stone Pillow: The Life and Times of Jona Lerman*. Globus Books, 1999. This memoir by a Polish immigrant to Palestine in 1934 illustrates the experiences of the early Zionists in Israel.

Tony McAleavy, *The Arab-Israel Conflict*. Cambridge, UK: SIGS Books, 1998. Well-explained history and consequences of the strife between Arabs and Jews in Israel.

Daniel J. Schroeter, *Israel: An Illustrated History*. Oxford, England: Oxford University Press, 1999. Thorough and well-illustrated history of Israel from biblical times, but with an emphasis on the modern nation.

Maida Silverman, *Israel: The Founding of a Modern Nation*. New York: Dial Books, 1998. Very readable history of the founding of Israel.

WEBSITES

ArabNet (www.arab.net). Good site, with many links, for information from an Arab perspective.

BBC News Online (www.bbc.co.uk). Good source for current news about Israel.

iGuide (www.iguide.co.il). Very thorough guide to Internet links on all aspects of Israel.

MideastWeb (www.mideastweb.org). This excellent site, promoting tolerance and peace in the Middle East through understanding and education, includes information and articles on Israel as well as many good links.

WORKS CONSULTED

BOOKS

Pam Barrett, ed., *Insight Guide: Israel.* New York: Langenscheidt, 2000. One in an acclaimed series of books about countries designed for both travelers and those interested in the culture of a country.

Ahron Bregman and Jihan El-Tahri, *Israel and the Arabs.* New York: TV Books, 2000. Based on a television documentary series, this book is an eyewitness account of journalists in the Middle East.

Daniel Jacobs, *Israel and the Palestinian Territories: The Rough Guide.* London: Rough Guides, 1999. One in a series of volumes designed for travelers, with good background information and insights about places and people in Israel.

Benny Morris, *Righteous Victims: A History of the Zionist-Arab Conflict, 1881–2001.* New York: Vintage Books, 2001. An outstanding and evenhanded account of the origins and development of the conflict between Palestinian Arabs and Jews.

Wendy Orange, *Coming Home to Jerusalem: A Personal Journey.* New York: Touchstone Books, 2000. This book, a series of essays based on the author's six years in Israel, discusses the lives and thoughts of Israelis from an insider's perspective.

Chaim Potok, *Wanderings: Chaim Potok's History of the Jews.* New York: Fawcett Crest Books, 1978. An imaginative and creatively told account of the history of the Jews from the time of Abraham through modern times, by an acclaimed writer of fiction.

Dennis Prager and Joseph Telushkin, *Why the Jews? The Reason for Anti-Semitism.* New York: Touchstone Books, 1983. Excellent and readable discussion of the origins and continuing power of anti-Semitism around the world.

George Robinson, *Essential Judaism: A Complete Guide to Beliefs, Customs, and Rituals.* New York: Pocket Books, 2000. A thorough one-volume compilation of information about Judaism, including reproductions of important historical documents.

Edward W. Said, *The End of the Peace Process: Oslo and After.* New York: Vintage Books, 2000. A discussion of the recent attempts at peace and why they have failed, by one of the most acclaimed writers on the Middle East.

Raymond P. Scheindlin, *A Short History of the Jewish People.* Oxford, England: Oxford University Press, 1998. Good overview of Jewish history from biblical times to today.

Tom Segev, *One Palestine Complete: Jews and Arabs Under the British Mandate.* New York: Henry Holt, 1999. Very readable history of the early years of the Jewish and Arab conflict in Palestine.

David K. Shipler, *Arab and Jew: Wounded Spirits in a Promised Land.* New York: Penguin Books, 2002. This book by a Pulitzer Prize–winning author focuses on cultural differences and prejudices of Arabs and Jews, and how these have contributed to the situation in Israel today.

Avi Shlaim, *The Iron Wall: Israel and the Arab World.* New York: W.W. Norton, 2001. A thorough, thoughtful discussion of how Israel's concerns about its own survival have resulted in policies that keep it continually at risk.

Joseph Telushkin, *Jewish Literacy: The Most Important Things to Know About the Jewish Religion, Its People, and Its History.* New York: William Morrow, 1991. An encyclopedia of information about essential aspects of Judaism and the Jews.

Leo Trepp, *A History of the Jewish Experience.* Springfield, NJ: Behrman House, 2001. This book traces the history of the Jews, with an emphasis on the Diaspora and modern times.

Dick Winter, *Culture Shock Israel.* Portland, OR: Graphic Arts Center Publishing, 1998. An amusing and informative portrait of what is unique about life in Israel.

WEBSITES

Ha'Aretz Online (www.haaretzdaily.com). Online edition of one of the top Israeli newspapers published in English; contains detailed information beyond that of foreign newspapers and has many links.

Israel (www.israel.org). Official government website maintained by the Israeli Ministry of Foreign Affairs; contains outstanding links to other sources as well as basic information about Israel.

Jerusalem Post Online (www.jpost.co.il). Another online edition of one of the top Israeli newspapers published in English.

Jewish History Resource Center (http://jewishhistory.huji.ac.il). An excellent site for information about all aspects of Jewish history and politics, maintained by Hebrew University in Jerusalem.

World Factbook: Israel (www.cia.gov/cia/publication/factbook). Statistical information compiled and distributed by the Central Intelligence Agency.

Yahoodi (www.yahoodi.com) A limited but good source for information about Israeli and Jewish history and the peace process.

INTERNET SOURCES

Matthew Hogan, "The 1948 Massacre at Deir Yassin Revisited," *The Historian*, Stanford University, Winter 2001. www.stanford.edu.

Israeli Ministry of Foreign Affairs, "Fifty Years of Hebrew Song," 1998. www.mfa.gov.il.

Laura King, "Passover Attack Memories Still Fresh," *Your Miami Everything Guide*, April 27, 2002. www.miami.com.

INDEX

PICTURE CREDITS

ABOUT THE AUTHOR

Laurel Corona lives in Lake Arrowhead, California, and teaches English and humanities at San Diego City College. She has a master's degree from the University of Chicago and a Ph.D. from the University of California at Davis. Dr. Corona has written many other books for Lucent Books, including *Afghanistan, Ethiopia, Life in Moscow, Peru,* and *The World Trade Center.* She has traveled extensively in Israel.